Religion and
Environmental Crisis

Edited by

Eugene C. Hargrove

Religion and Environmental Crisis

The University of Georgia Press

Athens and London

© 1986 by the University of Georgia Press
Athens, Georgia 30602

Designed by Kathi L. Dailey
Set in 10 on 13 Merganthaler Trump Mediaeval
Typeset by The Composing Room of Michigan, Inc.

The paper in this book meets the guidelines for
permanence and durability of the Committee on
Production Guidelines for Book Longevity of the
Council on Library Resources.

Printed in the United States of America

90 89 88 87 86   5 4 3 2 1

Library of Congress Cataloging in Publication Data

Religion and environmental crisis.

Papers presented at a colloquium held at the
University of Denver made possible by a grant from
the Phillips Foundation of Minneapolis through the
University of Denver's Center for Judaic Studies.
    Bibliography: p.
    Contents: Introduction / Frederick Ferré—Pan /
J. Donald Hughes—A native American
environmental ethic / Gerard Reed—[etc.]
    1. Human ecology—Religious aspects—
Congresses. 2. Human ecology—Moral and ethical
aspects—Congresses. I. Hargrove, Eugene C.,
1944–   . II. Phillips Foundation of Minneapolis
(Minn.) III. University of Denver. Center for
Judaic Studies.
GF80.R45 1986   174'.9333   86-7019
ISBN 0-8203-0845-5 (alk. paper)
ISBN 0-8203-0846-3 (pbk.: alk. paper)

To Eleanor Mae Lade Hargrove

Contents

Contents

Preface

Eugene C. Hargrove

Religion and Environmental Ethics: Beyond the Lynn White Debate

Until the early seventies environmental ethics was something that only environmentalists talked about. If you had asked a philosopher what he knew about the subject, you would most likely have been greeted by stunned silence, followed by a few tentative questions about what such a term could possibly mean. Environmental ethics was entirely alien to the normal kinds of things that philosophers talked about, and as a result they had no idea how to proceed.

Gradually, over the last fifteen years, however, environmental ethics has become a more professional subject as philosophy itself has begun to take an applied approach to contemporary issues. There are still questions, nonetheless, even today about the status of the field. Whether environmental ethics is considered professional or even important actually depends in large measure upon the standpoint of the individual making the assessment. If the standpoint is a philosophical one, the individual will make his or her judgment within the context of the "pure/applied" debate. "Pure" philosophers will most probably declare environmental ethics to be something akin to a cancerous infection, likely to destroy not only philosophy, but Western civilization as well. "Applied" ethicists, on the other hand, will speak not only of its value to the solution of critical social problems facing humankind today, but of its importance in correcting the errors of traditional philosophy, Greek and Early Modern, which has badly misunderstood both the nature of the natural world as we encounter it in experience and the relationship of fact and value to that world.

While the "pure" reaction to environmental ethics is, of course, highly charged emotionally and currently very hard to ignore, it should, nevertheless, not be viewed as a matter of serious concern—for such reactionary criticism is merely the traditional manner in which all innovations in professional philosophy are greeted. Consider, for example, the analytic/nonanalytic debate that preceded this one. To paraphrase Shakespeare, it was a battle full of sound and fury, but signifying nothing. Indeed, I cannot think of one useful thing that came out of that debate. Moreover, when the histrionics were over, it was clear that both sides had more in common than they had ever imagined—they were simply working on the same set of problems in slightly different ways. Likewise, when the pure/applied debate has run its course, it should become obvious to all that applied ethics is merely a natural and normal reaction to the excesses of emotivism earlier in this century, and a significant contribution not only to philosophy, but to human civilization as a whole.

A far greater problem is the reaction of the environmentalist, the government policy maker, the businessman, and the citizen concerned with environmental issues, for environmental ethics has already become so technical that many people now find it hard to follow the arguments; some even find the arguments unintelligible. The reason for this difficulty is not so much that philosophers are doing something wrong, but rather that the history of ideas out of which environmental concern developed in the nineteenth century was independent of almost any philosophical influence, and this concern was carried forward into the twentieth century largely in terms of a set of only vaguely articulated intuitions without any philosophical foundations. The "lay" interest in environmental ethics gradually developed out of a disquieting feeling that these intuitions were not properly supported, analyzed, or justified. What applied philosophers have provided, however, has not for the most part been what was initially expected and has not, therefore, removed the disquietude and uncertainty that most people feel about their environmental attitudes. Some even seem to regret that they called upon philosophers to get interested in environmental issues at all.

Despite this dissatisfaction, nevertheless, it is not very difficult to argue that much of value has been accomplished in environmental ethics over the last decade. If one looks back, for example, to William Blackstone's anthology *Philosophy and Environmental Crisis*, published in 1974, it is clear that the authors in that volume did not distinguish ethical issues relating to animal welfare and those relating to the environment. Since the appearance of J. Baird Callicott's "Animal Liberation: A Triangular Affair," published in *Environmental Ethics* in 1980, however, the issues have been sharply distinguished and a great deal of confused thinking eliminated. Although the separation of these issues seemed at first to place animal liberation and environmental ethics in warring camps, the trend today is to treat them as complementary, rather than antagonistic, approaches to parallel, and only slightly overlapping, sets of moral problems.

In addition to this very significant clarification, environmental ethics has also provided a valuable critique of the "rights" arguments commonly advanced by environmentalists and animal liberationists in this century. Environmental ethicists have been almost universally critical of such arguments, insisting that only individuals and more particularly moral agents should be considered rights bearers and that some other conceptual formulation should be developed to account for the moral status and/or moral considerability of nonhuman animals and nature that do not otherwise qualify. At present the most likely candidate to replace environmental and animal rights is intrinsic value, and the key issue in the ongoing debate seems to be whether moral considerability should be grounded in intrinsic value which is anthropocentric or, more radically, nonanthropocentric—that is, independent of our human valuational framework. When the dust clears, it should then be a simple task to correct the improper emphasis on instrumental value which has dominated environmental decision making, and indeed nearly all ethical behavior in this century.

Pointing to the progress that is being made in environmental ethics, nevertheless, is probably still not going to remove all the dissatisfaction that environmentalists and many other people feel. There are at least two reasons why this is the case. First of all, the work being done in environmental ethics is primarily theoretical and does not translate into simple guidelines that tell people what they ought to do—they still have to decide what to do on their own. Second, the principles developed by environmental ethicists do not command or compel people to be environmentally moral. Although environmental ethics is fundamentally concerned with justification, it is not really focused on persuasive arguments. As a result, it is no more able to handle the skeptical question "But why should I be moral?" than traditional ethics is. To deal with fundamental problems of motivation we must go beyond environmental ethics and deal with world views, and it is here that religion has an important role to play.

The importance of religion as a foundation for moral behavior has been obvious down through the centuries. It has been so important in fact that in periods of religious skepticism the role of religion in supporting morality has often been the front-line argument in defense of religious institutions and beliefs. Environmental ethics has not been an exception to this general trend. Many people interested in environmental affairs have already taken religion into account to some degree. The writings of Emerson, Thoreau, and John Muir, which are important in the history of the environmental movement, all have a religious dimension. This is even true of the writings of Aldo Leopold, considered by many to be the twentieth-century father of environmental ethics. Although Leopold's essay "The Land Ethic" is usually taken as a call for philosophy to become involved in environmental affairs, Leopold himself was just as concerned about religion. As Leopold put it: "No important change in ethics was ever accomplished without an internal change in our intellectual emphasis, loyalties, affections, and convictions. The proof that conservation has not yet touched these foundations of conduct lies in the fact that philosophy and religion have not yet heard of it." In this context, there is an important place for both philosophy and religion, for while philosophy may be better at analyzing ethical behavior (the intellectual emphasis), religion is much more effective at changing loyalties, affections, and convictions.

A decade ago no one would have doubted that religion had a central role in environmental ethics, for at that time religion was itself a central issue. The debate of the time was focused on an article by Lynn White, Jr., "The Historical Roots of our Ecological Crisis," which appeared in *Science* in 1967. White's thesis was that Christianity was responsible for the environmental crisis and that the Christian religion would either have to be altered significantly or abandoned entirely if we were ever to solve our environmental problems. White recommended that we improve Christianity by adopting the view of nature held by Saint Francis of Assisi, making him the patron saint of ecology. If that proved impossible in practice, he suggested that we look into the possibility of replacing Christianity with a non-Western religion, for example, Zen Buddhism.

Although the debate over the Lynn White thesis appeared at the time to be therapeutic, cleansing, and basically healthy, in retrospect it was not. Since almost no one was willing to accept either of his alternatives, the general response to White's position was overwhelmingly defensive, if not reactionary. The reactions of John Cobb, Jr., and John Passmore, a theologian and a philosopher respectively, illustrate the problems that arose.

Cobb in his book *Is It Too Late? A Theology of Ecology*, published in 1972, accepts White's basic position that Christianity is responsible for the environmental crisis, but he argues that non-Western views of nature, for example, North American Indian and Oriental religious views, which are generally more in harmony with nature, have not in practice proved to be any more effective in preventing environmental crisis than Christian ones. Despite their environmentally progressive attitudes, Indians still abused their environment from time to time, and deforestation took place in the East in exactly the same way as it did in the West. Cobb therefore recommends that Christianity be improved by placing emphasis on passages in the Bible more compatible with modern ecological and environmental attitudes. Unable to embrace Saint Francis as the patron saint of ecology, he substitutes Albert Schweitzer's views on reverence for life and attempts to ground ecological Christianity in Whitehead's process philosophy, a commendable project but one unlikely to capture the imagination or understanding of ordinary people, because of the complexity of process thought.

John Passmore, in *Man's Responsibility for Nature*, published in 1974, agrees with Cobb that non-Western religions are useless in improving Western environmental attitudes or in developing an environmental ethic, but he goes on to argue that Christianity is equally useless even if reinterpretation along the lines suggested by White and Cobb is undertaken. According to Passmore, so many contradictory things have been said in the history of Christianity and Western civilization as a whole that it is actually possible to find support for almost any kind of view anyone wants to advance—and this ability to justify anything ultimately amounts to the ability to justify nothing.

Passmore is actually opposed to any involvement of religion and non-Western philosophy in environmental affairs, and the possibility that an environmental ethic might be grounded in them is for him a good reason for abandoning the search for an environmental ethic altogether. Passmore begins his book, in fact, with a criticism of Aldo Leopold on religious grounds. Associating Leopold's *Sand County Almanac* with the Lynn White thesis, via an anonymous editorial in the *New Scientist*, Passmore concludes that the adoption of a "land ethic" must also require the abandonment of Christianity and indeed our Western traditions. Having established this point to his own satisfaction, Passmore goes on to attack environmental ethics throughout the rest of the book as being incompatible with the continuation of Western civilization as such. Thus, in moving from Cobb to Passmore, we find a rejection not only of a role for Eastern religion, but of one for Western religion as well.

There is much to commend in Lynn White's analysis, for undoubtedly Christianity did have some effect on our environmental attitudes. For example, White is certainly correct in claiming that the spread of Christianity was accompanied by the desacralization of nature, thereby opening the way for modern resource exploitation. It is also true that Christianity can take a great deal of credit for the development of modern science and technology, both of which have contributed to the environmental crisis in the twentieth century, if for no other reason than that the late-medieval Christian church was then functioning as a funding source comparable to the National Science Foundation of today. Likewise, Christianity with its asceticism and emphasis on the transcendence of God greatly inhibited the development of an aesthetic appreciation of nature, which is now so central to our basic attitudes toward nature and natural things.

Nevertheless, there is also good reason to lament the attention which the Lynn White thesis received throughout the last decade, for by blaming Christianity and by advocating what came to be regarded as radical and dangerous solutions to the environmental crisis, White had unwittingly shaped the debate in a way that ensured that there would be no useful outcome from it. The Lynn White thesis could not really be refuted, since in general the thesis was correct and as a result, critics could never find a decisive error that could draw the discussion away from it and onward in another direction. The result has been that for more than a decade the debate over the role of religion has gone nowhere, beginning and ending inconclusively with the same set of issues.

In theory at least, the debate could have proceeded differently. Consider, for example, the influence of Garrett Hardin's "Tragedy of the Commons," published only one year after White's piece. Like White, Hardin provided a startling thesis, calling for "mutual coercion, mutually agreed upon," which seemed to suggest dangers not only for the future of Western political institutions, but for Western civilization as a whole. Indeed, Passmore portrayed these issues on the same level on the Richter scale as the religious ones raised by White. Yet, as time has shown, they were not. Today, although it is, of course, common to begin a talk about environmental ethics in terms of the "tragedy of the commons," the discussion need not start there and it most certainly will not end there.

In retrospect, it would probably have been better if the Lynn White debate had never occurred. Had the discussion of the relation of religion and environmental ethics not been focused on the Christian blame or on the effectiveness of Eastern religions and philosophies as environmental replacements for Christianity, then we might have seen a period of fruitful comparative study of world religions aimed not at finding the best religion for everyone to adopt, but rather at finding ways for major religions to respond to the environmental crisis. In such a context, the emphasis would not have been on blame or replacement, but on constructive borrowing.

We cannot travel the same circular road forever. If there was a final and correct resolution to the Lynn White debate, we would have found it long ago. We must, therefore, following Wittgenstein's recommendations, both early and late, dissolve rather than solve this issue and move on to new ones where progress can be made. The way out of this fly bottle is the way we came in.

When we finally move beyond the Lynn White debate, it will then be possible for a rich period of comparative study to begin. For it to be a truly fruitful period, however, we must leave behind much of the baggage acquired during the Lynn White debate. Most important, Westerners must stop defending themselves against the perils of non-Western religion and philosophy. As Passmore noted in *Man's Responsibility for Nature*, a new ethic "is not the sort of thing that one can simply decide to have; 'needing a new ethic' is not in the least like 'needing a new coat.' A 'new ethic' will arise out of existing attitudes, or not at all." Although Passmore intended these remarks as part of his argument that comparative study should be avoided, if he is correct, then they are really part of an argument that such comparative study poses no threat at all. It is indeed just as inconceivable that some other religion will replace Christianity in the West as it is that Christianity will at this late date replace the religions and philosophies of the East. Perhaps comparative study will provide a basis for constructive borrowing to the benefit of both East and West. At a minimum such study by demonstrating alternative positions should facilitate independent tinkering within both Eastern and Western traditions. In any case it should help us get beyond worrying about the illusory threat to Western civilization posed by Eastern thought to the real threat to human civilization as a whole posed by the environmental crisis. If non-Western religion and philosophy can help, it is time we found out. This should be the task of comparative work in environmental ethics.

This volume is intended as a first step in that direction. It was not developed in accordance with any definite plan, structure, or theme. Rather, my intention was to create the broadest and most diverse body of new material possible. The book has its beginnings in a call for papers for a conference eventually held at the University of Denver. After the conference additional papers published in *Environmental Ethics* were added. All of the papers were refereed either for the conference or the journal. None were invited. They therefore represent an objective sampling of current work in the area of religion and environmental ethics, reflecting both new directions and the need for much additional work. The book provides discussions of a number of religious perspectives which rarely receive attention in a general anthology: Roman Catholicism, Judaism, Islam, the Native American perspective, and even pre-Christian Greek polytheism. Despite the diversity of perspectives presented, the volume is, nevertheless, unavoidably strongest in its representation of Protestant Christian work and weakest in its treatment of Far Eastern religion, for such is the current state of affairs in the comparative study of the role of religion in environmental ethics. This situation, however, is one which should soon be rectified as we finally move beyond the Lynn White debate. It is my hope that this book will do its part in bringing about a new beginning in this important and fascinating area of study.

Acknowledgments

Most of the papers in this volume were presented at a colloquium entitled "Ethical Issues of the Environment: Some Religious Perspectives," held at the University of Denver and made possible in part by a grant from the Phillips Foundation of Minneapolis through the University of Denver's Center for Judaic Studies. To broaden the scope of the original set of papers they have been supplemented with three additional papers, Susan Power Bratton's "Christian Ecotheology and the Old Testament," Iqtidar H. Zaidi's "On the Ethics of Man's Interaction with the Environment: An Islamic Approach," and John B. Cobb, Jr.'s "Christian Existence in a World of Limits," all of which have appeared previously in the journal *Environmental Ethics*. One paper, Po-keung Ip's "Taoism and the Foundations of Environmental Ethics," was presented at the conference and subsequently published in *Environmental Ethics*. The editor is grateful to the Phillips Foundation of Minneapolis and the University of Denver's Center for Judaic Studies for their generous support of the conference, to Holmes Rolston, III for editorial assistance with one of the manuscripts, and to Susan Power Bratton for assistance in the creation of the selected bibliography.

Frederick Ferré

Introduction

Many readers opening this book will be reminded of the earlier volume, *Philosophy and Environmental Crisis* (Athens: University of Georgia Press, 1974), edited by William T. Blackstone. This is appropriate since that pioneering work participated in the establishment of the then emerging field of reflective environmental studies—a field offering approaches to these urgent issues with the tools not of science but of ethical, religious, historical, or metaphysical thinking. This is the field to which this current offering is also addressed. The Blackstone book, made up of papers prepared for a conference held at the University of Georgia in February 1971, was in many ways a "first generation" contribution. The present volume may now be seen, after over a decade of lively discussion among philosophers, theologians, and scholars of religion, as "second generation"—or even "third generation," so rapidly do changes occur these days.

Some of the more prominent changes since early 1971 can be expressed negatively. For one thing, it is now not at issue that there *is* an issue for theologians and philosophers to debate in depth. Books as well as articles have been pouring from the presses. At least one professional journal, *Environmental Ethics*, was established during the period, with more in prospect. Graduate and undergraduate programs have blossomed in various parts of the country. The American

1

Theological Society has devoted an annual meeting to these fundamental questions.

Second, all this activity has made it clear to many that it is not eccentric for philosophers and theologians to take a lively professional interest in environmental questions. A decade ago it might have seemed that the issues, though real, were on the periphery. Now we are beginning to realize that all the central questions in theology and philosophy, from the nature of God to the understanding of creation to the meaning of history, and from the epistemology of science to the metaphysics of society, are implicit in the questions that must be asked and answered when confronting the environmental crisis in depth.

Nor, in the third place, is this discussion any longer exclusively tied to the enormously influential challenge thrown to Christian theologians by the article by Lynn White, Jr., "The Historical Roots of Our Ecologic Crisis," originally published in *Science* in early 1967 and widely reprinted, quoted, rebutted, and discussed. That discussion rumbled on throughout the decade of the 1970s, and there are (appropriately) a few echoes of it in the chapters that follow; but these essays have moved on with the now widespread recognition that the spiritual roots of our ecological crisis are more tangled than White's early spadework could have been expected to uncover.

A fourth change has been the recognition that the issues, even for thinkers, are not simply theoretical, but are deeply affective and motivational. To know the good is not always to do it. Ways of seeing and feeling, traditions of acting and reacting, are at issue at least as much as getting our concepts straight. That is why theology, which stands at the volatile surface between piety and philosophy, tradition and reform, needs now urgently to be invoked.

One of the noteworthy departures of this new book, for example, is the introduction of an important place for what may be called traditional pieties in contrast and in addition to the quest for novel theoretical frameworks. The various gradations and interactions are well represented here. J. Donald Hughes offers us a glimpse of Pan, and of what environmental ethics might be like in a polytheistic context not yet touched by biblical concepts or perceptions. In so doing, he attempts to make the concrete experience of Pan's pipes resonate again for us; he helps us to feel what it might be like to sense nature as sacred.

Something similar is done by Gerard Reed in his "homily" on Black Elk. The emphasis is on one concrete form of spirituality that was a real possibility for human beings to attain and sustain simply, without elaborate theological theorizing. It also is offered as a contrast to the dominant religious tradition of our civilization.

With like focus on the concrete pieties, but now with concern for the biblical heritage within which both Christianity and later Christendom were set, Jonathan Helfand provides a picture of Judaism and environmental ethics in which the Bible is seen as a source and record of personal piety toward nature, not as a theological textbook. All this lore, including the contrasts and similarities between the various simple, concrete religious approaches to the natural order, is essential to intellectuals who sometimes need reminding that the religious phenomenon is not first of all a theoretical matter, but a matter of values, intensely held and comprehensively relevant.

Still, human beings are thinking creatures, and piety, however simple, generates at least stories and sometimes complex theories to help the sacred values of a faith be understood as grounded in the nature of things and connected to other important elements in the relevant life world of the pious community. At the level of story and image, Martin LaBar extends our sense of the biblical heritage through his meditation on the Bible as reflecting various sorts of values in nature. His study is not yet metaphysics, but it is more than personal piety. He shows briefly at the end how theory (in this case ethical theory) can be drawn from image and parable, but his is not primarily a work of theory. Susan Power Bratton is more self-consciously theological, and thus more theoretical, than LaBar, but she is still closely concerned with the "compatible" interweaving of biblical images—the picture of God as uniquely transcendent Creator by "word" and by "breath"; the picture of man as "God's representative," both distinct from and responsible for "ruling" nature; and the picture of nature as beautifully good (*tob*), blessed, and praising of its maker—as the scriptural basis for constructing Christian ecotheology.

Thought from the East is sometimes also theoretical, as is shown by Po-Keung Ip in a metaphysical account of Taoism. The Tao Té Ching is cited, as ground and authority, but our author attempts to get beyond Lao Tzu's "mystical and poetical language" to specify more precisely what the images of piety offer in their "rich but at times amorphous representation." In this essay we find the culmination of an inner dynamic of religious thinking, from image to abstraction, that makes easy generalizations about the relationships between theology and philosophy difficult to defend.

Deductive reasoning is used to derive ethical principles needed to guide human uses of the environment by Iqtidar H. Zaidi from the Islamic tradition, and by Sophie Jakowska from the Roman Catholic. It is instructive to link these two essays, despite the obvious differences in their religious perspectives, because they both manifest the same kind of reasoning—to moral principles from sacred authorities—and because they both offer substantially the same descriptions and prescriptions. The description is of humanity superior to nature; the prescription is that we be responsible to God and regard in an ethical spirit our "right," as Zaidi says, "to subdue nature and benefit from natural resources."

4

This theory of man's ontological distinctness from and axiological superiority over nature is accepted, with qualifications, by Robert H. Ayers in his invocation of the "Christian realist" position of Reinhold Niebuhr. The inescapably dialectical character of human transcendence, however, is emphasized in this attempt to explore the resources of recent Neo-Orthodox Protestant theology for guidance in shaping current environmental policies.

John Cobb, Jr., accepts "Christian realism" as a long step ahead of dominant American attitudes toward the environment, and supports it as more appropriate than either moral exhortation or revolution, but he finds it limited and in need of supplementation by eschatological expectations, no matter how "unrealistic." The discernment of Christ, the way of the cross, and the prophetic vision are also spiritual resources for an unsettled and unsettling future in which traditional responses, however sensible, may not be enough.

Finally, Jay McDaniel urges a "new vision" that would transform not only the piety, the images, and the ethical rules of contemporary Christians, but also the fundamental theoretical groundwork of Christian believing. His reform would replace the "substantialist" conception of reality, with its alienating implications, with a "process" understanding that is at once dynamic and organic. It would be, he argues, a transformation worthy of the major historical discontinuity through which we are now passing. As he ends, he points a direction and offers a hope, but no assurance, that Christian theology, and with it real religion in the new age we are entering, will move toward unprecedented ecological sensitivity.

Readers will turn to these essays for many reasons. There is an interesting contrast—not always quite what one might expect—between them regarding the transcendence and the immanence of the sacred and how the sacred should be defined (and felt). There is a parallel contrast between the representations of humanity. To what extent are we human beings also transcendent over or beyond nature, and to what extent are we fully immanent in natural process? Is there intrinsic value in nature? If so, what is its character and its source? If not, what (if anything) should restrain us from all-out exploitation of the earth? Are the grounds for the ethical constraints to be found within or beyond the realm of nature?

These and many more questions are dealt with, variously, in the chapters that follow. None, however, is more important than the question that haunts the religious quest in all ages and all cultures: Where is the power to heal the actual in the light of the ideal? If the Blackstone volume was a philosophical prolegomenon to the development of an environmental ethic, this book begins a thoughtful search for the sources of sacred power to move mankind to live ethically in our threatened world.

J. Donald Hughes

Pan: Environmental Ethics in Classical Polytheism

Among ordinary people in Greco-Roman times, the strongest motive for the practice of environmental ethics was surely the sense of an all-pervasive spiritual power in nature. Whether we call this perception animism or pantheism, it simply amounts to a feeling that one ought not to injure the living things that share the world with mankind, or alter the natural arrangement even of land and sea, because nature is divine. All the gods had aspects of nature about them; to this all modern students of ancient polytheism would agree. But when we ask which of the gods is preeminently the universal god of nature, most of the same students are scandalized by a tradition that asserts in reply that it is Pan, the hoofed, horned, hairy, horny deity who took pleasure in playing pipes and pursuing nymphs. How could a goat god be the cosmic spirit, the indwelling Creator? And yet this was indeed maintained by many poets, philosophers, and religious teachers in the centuries from the Golden Age of Athens to the triumph of Christianity, and even beyond that.

Modern mythographers, for the most part, have devalued this tradition, calling it late and the result of a learned but misunderstood etymology. The Greek word *pan* means

7

"all." The ancient writers, it seems, took the apparently transparent meaning of the god's name as an explanation of his origin and function. "Pan" was the "all-god," nature personified, to them.[1] But modern scholarship has demonstrated that the true derivation of the name *Pan* is from *paōn*, "the nurturer," "he who feeds the herds" of sheep and goats, and therefore "shepherd." A cognate word is *pastoral*, and there is no doubt that Pan was a pastoral god, the power to whom shepherds and goatherds appealed throughout classical antiquity. Euripides calls him "the steward of husbandry" and credits him with causing the birth of the ram with the golden fleece.[2] His special land was Arcadia, the archetypal home of herders. The attributes that support this side of Pan meet us everywhere in ancient art and literature, and not least of them is his own goatlike appearance. He was, as Farnell says, a "generative daimon who watches the herds,"[3] ithyphallic, half goat, half man. But was this really Pan's origin?

An undeniable and perhaps even stronger strand in the tradition makes him a god of the forests and mountains, nurturer and protector of wild beasts, a kind of male Artemis. Indeed, he was often associated with her or her Roman counterpart, Diana. In this role he takes hunters and fishers as his protégés, although as we shall see he did not give them carte blanche to kill his wild creatures; hunters had to be wary of his moods and wishes. He is identified with wild trees like the pine and plants like streamside reeds and meadow flowers. So much a forest god was he that the Romans made him the equivalent of their Silvanus and classed him with the *di agrestes*, the deities of the wild. Greek poetry gives him cliffs, caves, promontories, and the highest rocky crags as his haunts. Sophocles summons him "from the serrated ridge of snow-capped Cyllene,"[4] and the old Homeric Hymn says he "has for his share every snow-covered ridge, the towering summits of mountains, and sheer rock-slabbed steeps."[5] Pan's oldest attributes are seen here; he was originally a god of the wilderness.

But in denying that Pan was "really" a universal nature god, the mythographers of the last hundred years have gone beyond a laudable fascination with etymological accuracy and historical roots to commit themselves to the genetic fallacy. Whatever the origin of the Pan figure, and etymological mistake notwithstanding, classical antiquity did accept Pan as god of "all things" (ta panta, the closest the ancient Greek language comes to providing a word for what we would call the "natural environment"). Almost all ancient ideas about etymology were more or less wrong, but they were believed, and that makes them important to the history of thought. A strong and widely accepted tradition, even though founded on a mistaken view of word origins, still influenced the thought of the age in which it was current, and is certainly worth recognition and study.

We find the conception of the universal Pan or, as he was later to be known, Great Pan, in Plato's *Cratylus*.[6] The philosopher elaborates the etymological argument by interpreting *Pan aipolos* (Pan the Goatherd) as *pan aei polōn* (ever-mover of all). "Pan," he says, "is the declarer of all things and the perpetual mover of all things." Other writers added the direct identification of Pan with all of nature. Reinforcing this line of thought was the existence of another Greek pun. The word *hyle* meant "wood" in both its English senses ("lumber" and "forest")[7] and also "substance" or the *prima materia* of the universe. Pan was called "Lord of the Forest" (*ho tēs hylēs kyrios*), a title which could be, and was, interpreted as "not [only] the lord of the woods, but the ruler of universal material substance."[8]

A writer most influential in the higher development of the idea of Pan is Servius, who in his commentary on Vergil makes a point-by-point equation of Pan's attributes with the features of the natural world:

> Pan is a rustic god, formed in similitude of nature, whence he is called Pan, that is, *All:* for he has horns, like the rays of the sun and the horns of the moon; his face is ruddy, like the shining air; he has a spotted fawnskin upon his breast, like the sky with stars; his lower parts are shaggy, on account of the trees, shrubs, and wild beasts; he has goat's feet, to denote the stability of the earth; he has a pipe of seven reeds, resembling the harmony of the heavens, in which there are seven sounds; he has a crook, that is, a curved staff, like the year, which runs back on itself, because he is the god of all nature.[9]

Although this might seem to be only a scholar's clever flight, a purple passage buried in a learned commentary, it was constantly quoted and requoted in just about every standard handbook from Roman times down to the nineteenth century. There is no doubt that this kind of allegory appealed to the minds of the educated in Greco-Roman times. And we do not have to look far to find evidence that Pan was actually worshipped in his more universal guise, and thus made an impression on the popular mind.

There is still extant a ritual book from a mystical religious association or *thiasos* of this period, containing sacred songs, called the *Orphic Hymns.* One of these is directed to Pan. Although the hymn was probably kept secret as part of the celebrations of the Orphic-Dionysiac mysteries, it reflects commonly held beliefs even so, since the Orphic religion was widespread in the Roman Empire. All the hymns in the collection use designations and epithets of the gods from traditionally accepted mythology, and this one is no exception. It is worth translating here in its entirety:

> TO PAN (to be offered with mixed incense)
> I call Pan the powerful, shepherd of the whole universe,
> Sky, and sea, and all the kingdom of earth,

And deathless fire; for all these are Pan's care.
Come, happy, leaping, circling with the Seasons,
Goat-legged, enthusiastic, lover of ecstasy, dancing among the
stars,
Weaving the harmony of the cosmos into playful song;
From dread fantasies protect me, from the fears that awe
mortals.
Rejoicing at springs with goatherds and oxherds too,
Keen-eyed hunter, lover of Echo, dancer with nymphs,
Many your names: green power in all that grows, procreator of
all,
Ruler of the cosmos, healer, bringer of light, increase, and
harvest;
Cave-haunting, your temper to be feared, a true Zeus with
horns.
You make the wide-reaching plains of earth firm,
The deep-flowing water of the unresting sea obeys you—
The ocean that circles earth like a diadem—
And air, that gives nurturing breath to all living,
And lightest fire, whose eye looks down from the topmost sky;
The elements stay separate at your commands,
And every living creature takes its purpose from your plans;
You fill the needs of human beings throughout the infinite
cosmos.
Come, happy, ecstatic, enthusiastic, come to drink my
offerings,
Most holy, and lead my life to a good end,
And send your panic terror away to the ends of the earth.[10]

A number of points should be noticed. Pan is here worshipped as creative and motive power of universal nature,
the controller and arranger of the four elements, earth,
water, air, and fire. Each of the elements is named twice in
the hymn, and the second time they are mentioned in order
from heaviest and most central to lightest and outermost, in
the ancient cosmographic view. Pan is summoned as god of
all things. One phrase used of him in the hymn, *peridrome*

synthrone Orais, presents the picture of the goat-hoofed god in the center of the circling goddesses of the seasons, leading them in their dance. In his study of the iconography of Pan, Wilhelm Heinrich Roscher observes that in art he is often portrayed at the center of the zodiac with the constellations revolving around him.[11] The hymn expresses this popular conception in the word *astrodiaite,* "dancing among the stars."

In her excellent study of the literary image of Pan, Patricia Merivale distinguishes two ways in which Pan was presented by Greco-Roman writers.[12] The first is a philosophical view typical of the Stoics, who used the Pan symbol as an allegorical emblem of the universe. This offered a metaphor for their pantheism and their belief in the indwelling world-soul. I think that Pan must have seemed a good image for pantheism—indeed the pun is not altogether inappropriate. As a theology, pantheism is always in tension between the reality of the *kosmos* and the reality of the *theos,* the world-soul. Pan's goat half insists on the one and unites it with his god half, which insists on the other.

The second mode that Merivale distinguishes is religious and uses Pan as a name, along with others, under which to approach the world-soul itself in worship and mystical devotion. This is the Pan presented by the Orphic cult hymn. He "joins elements of the traditional popular beliefs to the abstract pantheistic conceptions of the philosophers."[13]

Let us turn to those traditional popular beliefs and see how they supported the practice of environmental ethics. Pan offers several illustrations of the way in which Greek and Greco-Roman polytheism instilled an attitude protective of nature. Although he is called *erēmonomos,*[14] which means "he whose custom it is to frequent the wilds," the Greek word permits another translation, "lawgiver of the wilderness," he who embodies and enforces the customs one ought to follow in wild places. Aeschylus says it is Pan, along with Apollo and Zeus, who hears the cry of falcons whose nest has been robbed and sends a terrible nemesis to punish those responsible.[15] Pan was known to protect young, small, or helpless animals; when newly born, he had been wrapped in a rabbit skin. He afforded protection to designated species in certain places; according to Pausanias, "On Mount Parthenius there are tortoises which are well fitted for making lyres of; but the men of the mountain fear to catch them, and will not allow strangers to do so either, for they hold that the tortoises are sacred to Pan."[16] This is certainly a good example of a case in which a particular belief had a direct effect on environmental practice; nevertheless, it does introduce a paradox in the ethics associated with Pan: his attitude toward hunting.

Traditionally Pan was a hunter, a slayer of wild beasts, which is how he got the spotted lynx pelt he wore. Not only is he linked in cult with the huntress-goddess Artemis, but he is even said to have given her the pack of hunting hounds that accompany her in iconography. Greek hunters dedicated their spears and javelins to Pan,[17] and it is clear that they thought him to be the god who should supply them with game, because in Pan's own country of Arcadia, when hunters returned empty-handed from the chase, they would whip Pan's image with onions.[18] Although this rite looks like a punishment, it was doubtless in origin a purification to remove the fault in the hunters or in their hunting ritual that had been responsible for their lack of success. Here we are face to face with a seeming contradiction in the psychology of early hunters that reaches back to the primal experience of mankind, and should be familiar to every student of ancient environmental ethics. To members of societies that lived by hunting, as distinguished from those who hunt merely to supplement their domesticated food sources or to kill the beasts that prey on their herds and crops, wild animals were endowed with powerful spirits that had to be treated with careful respect in order to gain their assent to be hunted. In addition, wild species had guardian deities, masters or mistresses of beasts, whose concern it was to protect their charges and see that those who hunted carelessly or were heedless of the sacred nature and rights of animals met with appropriately bad results, such as failure to find prey, or missing the kill, or losing various kinds of power or skill, or suffering sickness, accident, or death. Artemis and Pan were, in their origins, exactly such guardians of the animals. Since hunters wanted to gain their assistance in the hunt, this made the preparatory ceremonies and taboos that accompanied the hunt necessary. From looking upon these deities as those who must be propitiated by hunters for success, to seeing them as helpers in hunting, and finally to picturing them as quintessential huntress and huntsman, is an understandable process that occurred in the history of the Mediterranean lands. But in that development, the earlier religious archetypes of the primal hunter were preserved in the form of ritual and proscription. Thus, Pan the hunter could restrain hunters from killing too many animals or from hunting inside sacred space.

Many features of the natural world were treated as under Pan's protection and therefore were preserved. This was especially true of certain trees, groves of trees, and forests. Pines were Pan's special favorites, but there are references to oaks, cypresses, wild olives, and other trees sacred to Pan or his Roman personae, Faunus and Silvanus. Sometimes it was an individual tree that was so honored, such as the oak tree near the road between Tegea and Argos.[19] Often whole stands of trees were consecrated as the preserves of the god. There was a protected grove of Pan on Mount Lycaeus, for example.[20] These groves were carefully delimited and provided with safeguards by the civil governments in whose jurisdiction they lay. Penalties were provided in law for anyone who cut trees or gathered wood in a holy *temenos* or *tem-*

plum, or who tried to hunt, fish, plow, or otherwise alter the natural environment in such a place without proper authority and expiatory rituals. The lawbreakers could be caught by priests or by special guards appointed by the local authorities. Groves could be dedicated to any god, goddess, or hero, of course, and here Pan's sanctuaries must serve as appropriate examples of a very widespread practice. "People call them the holy spaces of the immortals, and never mortal lops them with the axe."[21]

We noted above an important primal attribute of Pan as god of all wild forests, like his Roman cognates Faunus and Silvanus. Pliny the Elder made that identification clear in these words: "We also believe that the Silvani and Fauns and various kinds of goddesses are as it were assigned to the forests from heaven as their own special divinities."[22] The goddesses here mentioned are the nymphs or dryads, the companions and lovers of Pan, who live as indwelling spirits of trees until "at last the life of the Nymph and of the tree leave the light of the sun together."[23] Ancient people must have sensed the numinous presence of Pan and the other forest sprites whenever they went into the woods, and therefore were more careful of how they treated the sylvan environment. They would not cut trees without apology to the god accompanied by sacrificial offerings, and herders of sheep and goats were well advised to be careful where they let their destructive charges wander and nibble. This is evident from a ceremony that formed part of the annual Roman celebration of the Parilia, which asked forgiveness for shepherds and goatherds who had pastured their flocks inadvertently in sacred places.

Here again an apparent inner conflict in the Pan archetype emerges: although he is god of forests and also goat god, goats are most destructive to forests. Indeed, the present denuded state of much of the Mediterranean landscape is the result of the ubiquitous goat grazing that prevented the regeneration of trees once the forest had been felled. That there should be an association of goats with forests in the ancient mind is understandable; they were always there, nibbling the little trees down to stubs, consuming the leaves of shrubs and lower tree branches, and climbing up to eat the foliage they could not reach from the ground. Pan is ambivalent to goats in mythology. He is their protector and the enabler of their increase; he shares their well-known mating proclivities. But he is also an attacker of goats, a demon who inspires panic in the herds just as much as he does in human hearts. And the usual sacrifice to Pan was a goat, sometimes offered with the formula,

> [I offer] to Pan who loves the rock
> This yellow, bearded goat,
> A horned creature to the horned,
> A hairy one to the hairy-legged,
> A bounding one to the deft leaper,
> A denizen of the woods to the forest god.[24]

One is reminded of the annual offering on the Acropolis of a goat to Athena, goddess of the olive tree that goats were known to harm. Could the offering of a goat to Pan be a kind of atonement for the damage done to forests? Possibly, but it is also likely that the association of the goat god with forests originated in the time when wild goats grazed in a state of natural balance within the ecosystem, their numbers controlled by predators, before mankind adopted the role of protector and systematic guide to grazing. Such an ancient pedigree for Pan is possible; in the earliest known villages of agricultural people, the skulls of goats were preserved, decorated, and honored.

Mountains were revered as the sacred places, the *topoi* of Pan. Most of the ones particularly identified with him in classical literature were in Arcadia: Mounts Parthenius (where the Athenian messenger met him), Lycaeus, Lampeia (which he shared with Artemis), and Elaius; the hill Skoleitas; and the Nomian Mountains (where he invented the pan-pipes). "Mount Maenalus is held to be especially sacred to Pan, so that those who dwell around it say that they can actually hear him playing his pipes."[25] Beyond Arcadia, there were places sacred to Pan on Parnassus, Chaon, Pentelicus, and many other peaks. All these received the respect the ancients generally accorded to sacred places in the wild. As we have noted, "He has every snowy crest and mountain peak and rocky crag for his domain."[26]

But above all, popular piety represented Pan as the hidden indwelling power of nature. His presence could be sensed or evoked in a number of ways in which nature resonates with human beings. One of these is the echo, which reminded every Greek who heard it of Pan. Echo was a nymph with an especially beautiful voice whom Pan had torn to bits like a Bacchic victim, and her wide-flung members, each of which retained the gift of song, had been accepted by Mother Earth wherever they fell. So Echo, who is in mythological terms an attribute of Pan, is a fitting figure of nature's resonance. Pan was heard in every wild sound that rang through the forest; the tapping of the woodpecker brought to mind the story that his mother was exactly that bird, Dryope. And he was music, too: the music of wild nature, the innate music that can be drawn from the reed. It was said that when the nymph Syrinx, trying to escape from Pan, changed into reeds, Pan gathered them, bound them together, and blew across them, calling forth the "sweet echoes from a pipe"[27] that ever afterwards shepherds would make, but that sometimes could be heard out-of-doors when no players were about. Pan taught Hermes how to play the pipes, and though he lost a musical contest with Apollo, his nymphs were nurses of the Muses, who filled the world with music, and his own aid was invoked by composers of songs.[28] Pan's music is not always or even primarily untroubled harmony, however. One must remember that "goat song" in Greek is exactly the word "tragedy."

Pan in nature was not only music but also a shouter who startled into terror, one who caused the "panic" that takes its name from him. His hour was the midday rest, and shepherds feared to rouse him then, because his awesome voice could shatter the calm in the god-haunted wilderness and cause madness. Panic is a "wild" thing, neither good nor evil. It can scatter enemies on the battlefield, as it did the Persians at Marathon and the Gauls at Delphi.[29] It frightened monsters and made the Titans flee from the gods. When Pan wished, he could strike an individual with trembling, frenzy, or epilepsy. But what a god sends, a god can heal, and Pan was known as a healer. When Athens and Troezen were smitten by a raging plague, Pan "showed to the Troezenian magistrates dreams which supplied a cure for the epidemic."[30]

The mention of dreams brings to mind another way in which Pan represents nature resonating with human beings. He reveals himself in dreams to those who sleep outdoors under trees, especially in sacred groves, and particularly during the noonday nap. This association is demonstrated by the fact that his image was placed next to those of Hypnos (Sleep) and Oneiros (Dream) in a temple in Sicyon.[31] Pan was known as a sender of nightmares, sometimes in the shape of a goat or satyr and often erotic. The ancients noticed that animals also are troubled by dreams. Not all dreams of Pan, however, were thought to be bad.[32] Some of them were true forecasts, and it is these that people would seek by sleeping under his holy trees. The first priestesses at Pan's own oracle in Arcadia and at the old oracle of Gaia (Mother Earth) in Delphi were his nymphs Erato and Daphnis.[33] The latter is a personification of the laurel tree, which was later identified with Apollo at the same place. It is said that Pan taught Apollo the art of prophecy. Pan's status as speaker in dreams and giver of oracles connects him with Hermes, the speech god, and caused Plato to identify him as a deity of eloquence.[34] The Roman Faunus gave dream oracles in sacred groves, too; the ritual included putting on a crown of leaves, the removal of finger-rings, chastity, abstinence, and sleeping on the fleece of a sacrificed sheep.[35]

Pan, however, rarely desired chastity and abstinence—quite the opposite. The forest beings with which he usually cavorted were satyrs, sileni, fauns, silvani, and centaurs, all of whom represent the natural sexuality that we associate with the animal side of human nature. This is why so many of these creatures of the imagination are, like Pan himself, shown part human and part beast. The close link with Dionysus is as unmistakable in art as it is in the Orphic hymn: Pan's activities are like Bacchic orgies. He and his companions are embodiments of ecstatic sexuality, constantly chasing the nymphs, dryads, naiads, and Dionysiac maenads that flee from them or, on rare occasions, allow themselves to be caught. Erato, Pan's priestess nymph, exhibits her nature in her name; she is the muse of the erotic. In Aristophanes' play *Lysistrata* the heroine makes clear what a feast of Pan involves: Bacchic reveling and the pleasures of Aphrodite.[36] And when after a long period of enforced sexual abstinence due to her women's strike for peace, the men of Athens approach her with the obvious signs of their frustration protruding before them, she asks, "Is this the god Pan's doing?"[37] No expurgation of Pan can successfully remove this element of untamed sexuality from nature.

Pan has a higher side, too, as noble as that of any Greek god. There was no Greek as city-loving as Socrates, who remarked, "I am a man of the city and the men who live in the city teach me things I can't learn from trees in the countryside."[38] But when he went out to a grove of trees on the banks of the Ilissos stream for a quiet morning's conversation with his young friend Phaedrus, he expressed his open admiration for the natural beauty of the scene, and at the end of the dialogue was moved to address a prayer to Pan: "Dear Pan, and all you other gods in this place, let me be beautiful within, and let what I have outwardly harmonize with what I am inwardly. May I always think that the truly rich person is the one who loves wisdom, and may I have only as much gold as a temperate man would carry with him."[39] At the beginning of the prayer, Socrates acknowledges the *topos*, the location within the natural world, the sacred space, and the ethic that he enunciates in this setting is a life style of moderation, one that would bring the worlds of outer and inner nature into harmony.

Pan is the archetype of the resonance of nature, that divine otherness which at the same time reflects something human beings find deep within themselves. As James Hillman expresses it, "Pan is god both of nature 'in here' and nature 'out there.' As such Pan is the bridging configuration who keeps these reflections from falling into disconnected halves where they become the dilemma of a nature without soul and a soul without nature."[40] Thus understood, Pan is the bridge across the chasm the later Pythagoreans created between *psychē* (the personality) and *sōma* (the body), and therefore between the inner life of individuals and the natural environment. Pan, however, was always god, and therefore always maintained the numinous quality of nature, never reducing it to familiarity. It was the power of nature he represented that called forth from the ancient polytheist a respect for the environment and a reluctance to mar or violate the natural order. This, the motive for environmental ethics that was most operative in the world of classical Greece and Rome, is found both in popular devotion and in the concept of Great Pan as universal god of nature that is found in literature and philosophy.

It was said that Great Pan was dead. This story, told by Plutarch, has proved through its many retellings to be one of the most fascinating and haunting to survive from antiquity.[41] A sailing vessel drifted in windless calm near the Isles of the Echinades when a voice was heard calling, "Thamus, Thamus!" This turned out to be the name of the ship's Egyptian pilot, and when he answered, the voice said, "When you come next to the marshes, announce that Great Pan is dead." He did so, and heard in response "a great cry of lamentation, not of one person, but of many, mingled with exclamations of amazement." Plutarch tells us this happened in the time of Tiberius Caesar, and later writers connected it with the crucifixion of Jesus Christ, which took place in the same reign. The coincidence marks an important watershed in the history of thought about the environment. Pan died when Christianity arose, and the view of nature he stood for died too. Greco-Roman polytheism was from the beginning a religion that sacralized nature, and its eradication and/or absorption by Christianity involved the death of the personification of nature's indwelling divine power, Pan, or his transmutation into the horned, goat-hoofed devil who represented nature now as a snare and a delusion to the faithful, whether it be nature within or nature "out there." As a result of the "death of Great Pan," the natural world lost its numinosity, its sacredness. The groves of speaking trees could now be cut down, in fact had to be destroyed so that naïve peasants would no longer hear voices in the leaves. Mountains became heaps of nonliving stones where an unseen musician no longer piped. Animals once sacred to the god became mere "game" to be hunted for sport and served at feasts from which Bacchus—even if not his product—was carefully excluded. Nothing in the created world resonated in the old way any longer. Echo had been banished. In such a world, human beings were free, except for what check the doctrine of stewardship might afford, to use their power to change natural resources into their own creations, to modify the natural arrangement of things, to kill and to pollute. One need not say much more in this vein, because what followed in history has been well described by Lynn White, Jr., and others.[42]

It is intriguing, nevertheless, to ponder what might have happened if Great Pan had not died. At the time that ancient polytheism was suppressed, it was showing signs of developing into an inclusive pantheistic monotheism. This tendency can be seen in the most important philosophical movements in the first three centuries of Imperial Rome: Stoicism, Neo-Platonism, and the widespread and typical Eclecticism. The worship and allegory that presented Pan as the all-pervasive spiritual power in nature was one of the ways in which this process manifested itself. The development seems to have been in the direction of something like Hinduism's recognition of the One behind the many, with the continued affirmation of the sacredness of the natural order and respect for living things. Had that combination of religious syncretism and Greek rationalism continued, it is quite possible that an explicit environmental ethics might have developed in the West much earlier than it actually did, and it might have kept in balance the claims both of human nature and the natural environment.

Notes

1. Another explanation, given in the *Homeric Hymn to Pan*, 19.47, is that he is the one who delighted "all" the gods, especially Dionysus.
2. Euripides, *Electra*, 703.
3. Lewis Richard Farnell, *The Cults of the Greek States*, 5 vols. (Oxford: Oxford University Press, 1907), 5:431.
4. Sophocles, *Ajax*, 697.
5. *Homeric Hymn to Pan*, 19.6–7.
6. Plato, *Cratylus*, 408B–D.

7. His images were often of wood. See Pausanias, 1.36.2. A similar pun occurs on the Latin word *materia.*

8. Macrobius, *Saturnalia,* 1.22.3.

9. Servius, *Commentary on Vergil, Eclogues,* 2.31.

10. Translated by the author. The text used is that in *The Orphic Hymns,* text, translation, and notes by Apostolos N. Athanassakis (Missoula, Mont.: Scholars Press, 1977), pp. 18, 20.

11. Wilhelm Heinrich Roscher, *Ausführliches Lexicon der Griechischen und Römischen Mythologie* (Leipzig: Teubner, 1897), vol. 3, pt. 1, pp. 1467–68.

12. Patricia Merivale, *Pan the Goat-God: His Myth in Modern Times* (Cambridge, Mass.: Harvard University Press, 1969), p. 11.

13. Wilhelm Heinrich Roscher, "Pan als Allgott," *Festschrift für Johannes Overbeck* (Leipzig, 1893), pp. 56–72. The quotation in English translation is from Merivale, *Pan the Goat-God,* p. 9.

14. Nonnos, *Dionysiaca,* 14.68.

15. Aeschylus, *Agamemnon,* 54–58.

16. Pausanias, 8.54.5.

17. James George Fraser, *The Golden Bough: A Study in Magic and Religion* (New York: Macmillan, 1935), 1:6, n.4.

18. Theocritus, 7.106ff. and scholion.

19. Pausanias, 1.54.4.

20. Ibid., 8.38.5. See also Vergil, *Aeneid,* 8.601.

21. *Homeric Hymn to Aphrodite,* 5.267–68.

22. Pliny, *Natural History,* 12.2(3).

23. *Homeric Hymn to Aphrodite,* 5.271–73.

24. *Greek Anthology,* 6.32.

25. Pausanias, 8.36.8.

26. *Homeric Hymn to Pan,* 19.6–7.

27. Longus, *Daphnis and Chloe,* 2.29.

28. Aristophanes, *Thesmophoriazusae,* 977, *Frogs,* 229.

29. Herodotus, 6.105; Pausanias, 10.23.7.

30. Pausanias, 2.32.5.

31. Ibid., 2.10.2.

32. Artemidorus, *Interpretations of Dreams,* 2.37.

33. Pausanias, 8.37.11, 10.5.5.

34. Plato, *Phaedrus*, 263D.
35. Ovid, *Fasti*, 4.641.
36. Aristophanes, *Lysistrata*, 2.
37. Ibid., 998.
38. Plato, *Phaedrus*, 230D.
39. Ibid., 279B–C.
40. James Hillman and Wilhelm Heinrich Roscher, *Pan and the Nightmare*, ed. James Hillman (Irving, Tex.: Spring Publications, 1979), p. ix.
41. Plutarch, *Why the Oracles Cease*, 17; *Moralia*, 419B–D.
42. Lynn White, Jr., "The Historical Roots of Our Ecological Crisis," *Science* 155 (1967): 1203–7.

Gerard Reed

A Native American Environmental Ethic: A Homily on Black Elk

Along with Smokey the Bear and Henry David Thoreau, Native Americans have symbolized a certain environmental concern. Various observers have noted the ceremonies and customs that illustrated a reverence for Mother Earth and her creatures. Many, to be sure, found such ceremonies and customs quaint rather than exemplary, but a few gifted seers such as Thoreau (who devoted much time to reading and thinking on his never-written "Indian book")[1] actually saw the value and validity of tribal cultures' environmental concerns. More recently, some environmentalists have portrayed the Indians as arch-conservationists, and television spots have featured a tearful red man encouraging us to lament the anguish of our planet.

Thus, Americans acclaim the Indian as a native symbol of environmental sanity—although such elevation to ecological sainthood prods critics to decry exaggerated images of primitive purity. And the critics have a point: Native Americans, both past and present, lacked perfection, even in their celebrated love for nature. The Indian-as-ecologist, like the Indian-as-savage, is, in many ways, a stereotype, and stereotypes generally distort actualities. Yet, in this instance, one can at least argue that Native Americans developed a more sensitive, gentle, responsible environmental ethic than have the Europeans who succeeded them.

Making general statements about "Indians" or "Native Americans" is at best risky. One can write accurately only about cultural groups, for their languages and traditions vary immensely; but so long as generalizations are understood as such, so long as they are not pressed too far, they may encompass many North American tribal cultures.

For the purpose of this essay, let us explore a representative text in Black Elk's *The Sacred Pipe:* "We should understand well that all things are the works of the Great Spirit. We should know that He is within all things: the trees, the grasses, the rivers, the mountains, and all the four-legged animals, and the winged peoples; and even more important, we should understand that He is also above all these things and peoples. When we do understand all this deeply in our hearts, then we will fear, and love, and know the Great Spirit, and then we will be and act and live as He intends."[2] Implicit in this text are three ideas which I will examine in turn: that nature reveals the Creator, that creatures deserve respect, and that conservation reveals devotion.

Nature Reveals the Creator

That nature reveals the Creator is evident from Black Elk's claim that "all things are the works of the Great Spirit." Native Americans lived within a pervasively religious milieu. They set aside no special day for worship, for they devoted much time each day to prayer, considered fasting an important spiritual exercise, and frequently held religious dances. "Every dawn as it comes is a holy event, and every day is holy," Black Elk said, "for the light comes from your Father Wakan-Tanka."[3] Rather than building shrines or houses of worship,[4] they found in nature elevating places for their religious retreats and observances. According to Gerard Manley Hopkins, "The world is charged with the grandeur of God."[5] Similarly, from the standpoint of the Indian world view, virtually everything, every event, had a spiritual dimension. In this way, their environmental ethic and religious practices intertwined.

Like most preindustrial people, Native Americans rarely questioned the existence of a supreme being. They presupposed some sort of a creator, whose reality is amply evident in creation.[6] Native names for the Creator illustrate their understanding of his nature. To the Iroquois, *Manitou* meant "One who makes everyone's breath." Similarly, in Cherokee, *Ishtohoollo* meant "the great, beloved, holy Cause." For the Crow, *Ah-badt-dadt-deah* meant "the One-who-made-all-things." In Lakota, *Wakan-Tanka* meant "Great Mystery" or "Great Holy" or "Holy Mystery."[7]

In all languages, words mean more than translations convey. *Great Spirit,* often assigned to native notions of God, frequently failed to convey the full meaning of the terms used by the various Indian languages. Some more clearly mean "Creator" than others. Generally speaking, nevertheless, the better one grasps the meaning of the aboriginal word the more clearly it points to a Creator who called the whole world into being. As Black Elk indicated in prayer: "O Father and Grandfather *Wakan-Tanka,* You are the source and end of everything. My Father Wakan-Tanka, You are the One who watches over and sustains all life." He adds a few lines further on: "You are first and always have been! Everything belongs to You. It is You who have created all things! You are One and alone."[8]

The Creator, ultimately, is one. Despite a widespread notion that Indians were polytheistic (a notion too frequently spread by a series of observers who rarely learned native languages or entered into the native world view), many Indians

were, in the ultimate sense, pantheistic and even monotheistic. James Adair, who spent years among the south-
eastern Indians, insisted they worshipped "'the great, benefi-
cent, supreme, holy spirit of fire,' who resides (as they think)
above the clouds, and on earth also with unpolluted people."[9] George Catlin, who lived with the tribes of the north-
ern plains for nearly a decade, said that "in all parts" the
Indians worshipped "the Great Spirit, . . . instead of a plu-
rality of gods, as ancient pagans and heathens did—and their
idols of their own formation. The North American Indians,
are nowhere *idolaters*—they appeal at once to the Great
Spirit, and know of no mediator, either personal or sym-
bolical."[10] Frank Linderman, who lived for forty years
among the Crow, also insisted they were thoroughly monotheistic.[11] Certainly they believed in a vast array of subordinate powers and beings (somewhat akin to angels and devils
in Christianity), but they still believed in an ultimate source
of all things. This being was both transcendent and immanent, both "within all things" and "above all those things"
as Black Elk puts it.[12]

Sensing the Creator's immanence in all things made
Native Americans attentive to the land. If he is in everything, he can be excluded from nothing. If everything is in
him, nothing is apart from him. The immanent Spirit, by his
real presence in all things, makes all he dwells in (or all that
dwells in him) precious. While rarely expressed in theological language, the Native American's belief in the absolute immanence of the Creator in creation undergirds and
structures all his ethics.

Thus the Indians' love for and attachment to *place*. As
Vine Deloria asserts, Native Americans revered particular
places more than historic events.[13] Whether it be Bear Butte
in the Black Hills for the Sioux or the four sacred mountains
in the Southwest for the Navajo, important places revealed
truth about God. "From the time the Indian first set foot

upon this continent," N. Scott Momaday says, "he has centered his life in the natural world. He is deeply invested in
the earth, committed to it both in his consciousness and in
his instinct. In him the sense of place is paramount. Only in
reference to the earth can he persist in his true identity."[14]
As a result, treaties demanding land cessions, removal to re-
servations, and finally the allotment of land did more than
deprive Indians of their economic base—the treaties also
severed their ties to the Creator by detaching them from
their people's sacred sources of revelation.

The land and the plants and animals that flourished on
the land all revealed the nature of the Creator to those who
patiently awaited wisdom. Tatanga Mani (Walking Buffalo), a
Stoney Indian from Canada, said, "We saw the Great Spirit's
work in almost everything: sun, moon, trees, wind, and
mountains. Sometimes we approached him through these
things." He continues: "Did you know that trees talk? Well
they do. They talk to each other, and they'll talk to you if
you listen. Trouble is, white people don't listen. They never
learned to listen to the Indians so I don't suppose they'll listen to other voices in nature. But I have learned a lot from
trees: sometimes about the weather, sometimes about animals, sometimes about the Great Spirit."[15] Luther Standing
Bear, a Sioux, agrees: "Everything was possessed of personality, only differing with us in form. Knowledge was inherent in all things. The world was a library and its books were
the stones, leaves, grass, brooks, and the birds and animals
that shared, alike with us, the storms and blessings of
earth."[16]

Thus, nature was a source of divine revelation for Native
Americans. With insights derived from the study of Mother
Earth and her children, native thinkers understood the
Creator as mighty, holy, nurturing. They studied natural
beings, not so as to make them idols, but to use them as
lenses through which to peer into the depths of the Great

Mystery. Just as Christians revere the written Word of God, preserving and studying the Bible, Native Americans revered the created world, preserving and studying it as a manifestation of and message from God.

Creatures Deserve Respect

Creatures deserve respect because the Great Spirit "is within all things." Whether great or small, they are all bound together by the web of life spun by the Creator of all. Within that web, life must be taken to sustain life, but it must be done reverently and with restraint. Balance should be maintained with a sense of propriety and permanence. Unlike European immigrants who feared and sought to conquer the American "wilderness," the Indian felt at home in the world as designed by the Creator. As Luther Standing Bear recalls: "We did not think of the great open plains, the beautiful rolling hills, and winding streams with tangled growth, as 'wild.' Only to the white man was nature a 'wilderness' and only to him was the land 'infested' with 'wild' animals and 'savage' people. To us it was tame. Earth was bountiful and we were surrounded with the blessings of the Great Mystery."[17] Feeling at home in his world, Ohiyesa (Charles Eastman) put it this way: "The Indian loved to come into sympathy and spiritual communion with his brothers of the animal kingdom, whose inarticulate souls had for him something of the sinless purity that we attribute to the innocent and irresponsible child. He had faith in their instincts, as in a mysterious wisdom given from above; and while he humbly accepted the supposedly voluntary sacrifices of their bodies to preserve his own, he paid homage to their spirits in prescribed prayers and offerings."[18]

As Eastman indicates, many native hunters apologized to the animals they killed. After killing a bear, one chief,

Wawatam, conducted a ceremony wherein he lamented the necessity of killing a "friend."[19] According to Luther Standing Bear, "Kinship with all creatures of the earth, sky and water was a real and active principle. For the animal and bird world there existed a brotherly feeling that kept the Lakota safe among them and so close did some of the Lakotas come to their feathered and furred friends that in true brotherhood they spoke a common tongue."[20]

Such statements have often been taken to show how pantheistic or animistic Indians were. Yet, many of their own spokesmen seemed to believe in a Supreme Being, a Creator, who somehow stands above as well as within his creation. What they really believed, not what the deistic-tending Europeans who observed them concluded,[21] was that the Creator is so manifestly present in his creation that we dare not offend him by needlessly destroying or desecrating his world. Thus, the environmental ethic which grew out of Native American culture needs to be understood as an effort to live harmoniously with the Creator by living gently with other forms of life he has made and continuously sustains by his immanent presence.

Conservation Reveals Devotion

Conservation reveals devotion, because Indians should "be and act and live as He intends." Given their reverence for the Creator and his creatures, Native Americans generally lived according to an ethic of conservation. Before European contact, and even during the epoch of dislocation and removal, native spokesmen frequently expressed concern for the land that was undergoing destruction as the frontier raced westward. Their commitment to conservation often faded, as Calvin Martin shows so clearly in *Keepers of the Game*,[22] when European diseases devoured native populations and in

the process discredited the healing powers of traditional religion. Thus, religiously disillusioned Indians engaged in the
fur trade and became as rapacious as their white colleagues.
Yet, for all that, one finds a certain conservation conscience
in tribal traditionalists right up to the present.[23]

Pre-Columbian cultures generally lived wisely with the
earth. Properly practiced, the slash-and-burn technique of
woodlands Indians preserved the fertility of forested regions
in North and South America. Observers today still find that
the soil maintains its health in small pockets of Guatemala
and Peru where traditional, distinctively Indian-style agriculture endures and the people subsist on a broad variety of
foodstuffs.[24] Hunters certainly killed more than necessity
dictated, but for most Indians hunting was a "sacred voca-
tion,"[25] and its impact upon the abundant wildlife of the
Americas rarely endangered any species. European conquest
radically changed that, importing values that elevated material progress and prosperity over preservation of nature's
well-being. Evaluating that process, Vine Deloria, Jr., a
Sioux, comments: "In recent years we have come to understand what progress is. It is the total replacement of nature
by an artificial technology. Progress is the absolute destruction of the real world in favor of a technology that creates a
comfortable way of life for a few favorably situated people.
Within our lifetime the difference between the Indian use of
land and the white use of land will become crystal clear. The
Indian lived with his land. *The white destroyed his land. He
destroyed the planet earth.*"[26]

Such conservationist attitudes infused an ethic of moderation and self-restraint. Indians generally lived simply, emphasizing the value of sharing, condemning any hoarding of
possessions. They lived contentedly with the world the
Creator had made. As the great Nez Percé Chief Joseph said:
"We were contented to let things remain as the Great Spirit

made them. They [Anglo-Americans] were not, and would change the rivers and mountains if they did not suit them."[27]

A century later, a Cherokee named Jimmie Durham, representing the International Treaty Organization, spoke before a congressional committee holding hearings on the Endangered Species Act. His testimony focused on the question, who has the right to destroy a species? Drawing upon his Cherokee heritage, he began:

> In *Ani Yunwiyah*, the language of my people, there is a word for land: *Eloheh*. This same word also means history, culture and religion. This is because we Cherokees cannot separate our place on earth from our lives on it, nor from our vision and our meaning as a people. From childhood we are taught that the animals and even the trees and plants that we share a place with are our brothers and sisters.
>
> So when we speak of land, we are not speaking of property, territory or even a piece of ground upon which our houses sit and our crops are grown. We are speaking of something truly sacred.[28]

Citing the building of the Tellico Dam, which would flood historic Cherokee sites as well as threaten a small fish, the snail darter, Durham indicated that he was appalled by the attitudes of many politicians who would sacrifice land and fish to generate electricity and added, "It is this incredible arrogance towards other life that has caused such destruction in this country." He concluded:

> Who has the right to play God and judge the life or death of an entire species of fellow beings which was put here by the same power that put us here? Who has the right to destroy a species of life, and what can assuming that right mean?
>
> Let me be emotional: To me, that fish is not just an abstract "endangered species" although it is that. It is a Cherokee fish and I am its brother.[29]

The Tellico Dam, of course, was built despite Cherokee protests. Electricity triumphed over the snail darter. Consumption overwhelmed conservation. In truth, the moral restraint necessary to live in harmony with the earth rarely guides America. Nevertheless, it was central to the ethics of Native America, just as it was to the ethics of Saint Francis or E. F. Schumacher. As Ohiyesa (Charles Eastman) observed:

> The native American has been generally despised by his white conquerors for his poverty and simplicity. They forget, perhaps, that his religion forbade the accumulation of wealth and the enjoyment of luxury. To him, as to other single-minded men in every age and race, from Diogenes to the brothers of Saint Francis, from the Montanists to the Shakers, the love of possessions has appeared a snare, and the burdens of a complex society a source of needless peril and temptation. Furthermore, it was the rule of his life to share the fruits of his skill and success with his less fortunate brothers. Thus he kept his spirit free from the clog of pride, cupidity, or envy, and carried out, as he believed, the divine decree—a matter profoundly important to him.[30]

To conserve, to prolong, to maintain the health of Mother Earth, man must live temperately. Live simply. Live modestly. Share goods. Such temperance formed the heart of Native American environmental ethics. As Black Elk proclaimed: "Every step that we take upon You should be done in a sacred manner; each step should be as a prayer."[31] "Because You have made Your will known to us," he continued, "we will walk the path of life in holiness, bearing the love and knowledge of You in our hearts!"[32]

Conclusion

Traditional Native American thinkers such as Black Elk articulated an ethic of reverence for nature as the handiwork and manifestation of God. Religious values clearly informed ecological attitudes and practices and enabled this continent's first residents to live on and maintain the health of Mother Earth for many millennia. Consequently, as J. Donald Hughes says, "The condition of the New World as it met the 'eyes of discovery' was a testimonial to the ecological wisdom of the Indians, both their attitudes and their ways of treating the natural environment."[33]

Contemporary American environmentalists searching for an enduring ecological ethic will find in Native Americans reasonably recent, rather alluring, utterly American, examples of people who lived well with their world. Such comparative study has enabled J. Baird Callicott, for example, "to argue that the world view typical of American Indian people has included and supported an environmental ethic, while that of Europeans has encouraged human alienation from the natural environment and an exploitative practical relationship with it." It is thus possible to "argue that the North American 'savages' were indeed more noble than 'civilized' Europeans, at least in their outlook toward nature."[34] Pondering Black Elk's insights certainly confirms such views.

Notes

1. Robert F. Sayre, *Thoreau and the American Indians* (Princeton, N.J.: Princeton University Press, 1977).
2. Black Elk, *The Sacred Pipe*, ed. Joseph Epes Brown (New York: Penguin Books, 1973), p. xx.
3. Ibid., p. 7.
4. In the Southwest, however, circular kivas were constructed and served as religious centers.
5. Gerard Manley Hopkins, "God's Grandeur," in *Poems of Gerard Manley Hopkins* (New York: Oxford University Press, 1967), p. 66.
6. I will occasionally use a masculine pronoun to refer to the

Creator, though Indian thought often included the feminine as well as the masculine in the notion of supreme being.

7. James Adair, *Adair's History of the American Indians* (New York: Promontory Press, 1930), p. 48, explains the meaning of Ishohoollo; Frank Linderman, *Plenty-Coups, Chief of the Crows* (Lincoln: University of Nebraska Press, 1966), pp. 11, 80, describes the Crows' Ah-badt-dadt-deah.

8. Black Elk, *Sacred Pipe*, pp. 14, 46.

9. Adair, *History*, p. 20.

10. George Catlin, *Letters and Notes on the Manners, Customs, and Conditions of the North American Indians* (1844; reprint ed., New York: Dover Publications, 1973), 2: 232.

11. Linderman, *Plenty-Coups*, pp. 11, 80.

12. Black Elk, *Sacred Pipe*, p. xx.

13. Vine Deloria, Jr., *God Is Red* (New York: Grosset and Dunlap, 1973).

14. N. Scott Momaday, "I Am Alive," in *The World of the American Indian* (Washington, D.C.: National Geographic Society, 1974), p. 14.

15. Quoted in T. C. McLuhan, ed., *Touch the Earth* (New York: Promontory Press, 1971), p. 23.

16. Luther Standing Bear, *Land of the Spotted Eagle* (Lincoln: University of Nebraska Press, 1978), p. 194.

17. Ibid., p. 38.

18. Charles Eastman, *The Soul of the Indian* (Boston: Houghton Mifflin, 1911; reprint ed., New York: Johnson Reprint Corp., 1971), p. 15.

19. Alexander Henry, *Alexander Henry's Travels and Adventures in the Years 1760–1776*, ed. Milo Quaife (Chicago: R. R. Donnelly and Sons, 1921), p. 140.

20. Standing Bear, *Land of the Spotted Eagle*, p. 193.

21. Jürgen Moltman, in *The Trinity and the Kingdom* (New York: Harper and Row, 1981), insists that the Western Christians have been so concerned with the unity of God that they have effectively denied his triune nature. Western thinkers have, he insists, been largely deistic and thus removed God from creation.

22. Calvin Martin, *Keepers of the Game* (Berkeley and Los Angeles: University of California Press, 1978).

23. See such examples as *The Akwesasne Notes,* published by the Mohawks, the letter from Hopi elders to President Nixon, in *Touch the Earth,* pp. 170–71, and the North Cheyenne's concern for strip mining, in K. Ross Toole, *The Rape of the Great Plains* (Boston: Little, Brown, 1976), pp. 50–68.

24. For Guatemala, see Gerardo Budowski, "Middle America: The Human Factor," in *Global Perspectives on Ecology,* ed. Thomas C. Emmel (Palo Alto, Calif.: Mayfield, 1977), pp. 199–214; see Wendell Berry, *The Gift of Good Land* (San Francisco: North Point Press, 1981), pp. 3–46.

25. Martin, *Keepers of the Game,* p. 113.

26. Vine Deloria, Jr., *We Talk, You Listen* (New York: Macmillan, 1970), p. 186.

27. Quoted in Dee Brown, *Bury My Heart at Wounded Knee* (New York: Bantam Books, 1970), p. 304.

28. Quoted in Edwin Pister, "Endangered Species: Costs and Benefits," *Environmental Ethics* 1 (1979): 347–48.

29. Ibid.

30. Eastman, *Soul of the Indian,* pp. 9–10.

31. Black Elk, *Sacred Pipe,* p. 13.

32. Ibid., p. 14.

33. J. Donald Hughes, *American Indian Ecology* (El Paso: Texas Western Press, 1983), p. 3.

34. J. Baird Callicott, "Traditional American Indian and Western European Attitudes Toward Nature: An Overview," *Environmental Ethics* 4 (1982): 293.

Jonathan Helfand

The Earth Is the Lord's: Judaism and Environmental Ethics

The earth is the Lord's and the fullness thereof.

Psalm 24:1

The heavens are the Lord's heavens, but the earth he has given to mankind.

Psalm 115:16

The apparent contradiction between these two biblical verses troubled Jewish sages over a thousand years ago, and modern society still seems to be plagued by the dilemma they embody: to whom does the earth really belong and what are the consequences of holding such title?

For the past century and more, Western man has acted as master and lord of his environment, paying no heed to the effects of his actions on the environment. In the name of progress, water, land, air, and the wildlife they support have been despoiled and depleted, perhaps beyond reclaim, and in a manner unmatched in the annals of human history. Not all society was blind to this devastation. The outrage over man's rapaciousness, the demands for the protection and preservation of the environment, became more vocal and vehement as the corruption of nature grew in scope. Attacking this destructiveness, environmentalists sought to discover a cause for it, much as others had sought an excuse. For some, the nemesis of modern man turned out to be the biblical tradition itself.

The argument of these environmentalists was as follows. The pollution of the environment associated with the advance of the industrial revolution and the recklessly extravagant consumption of nature's irreplaceable treasures could all be traced to one cause: the rise of monotheism. The doctrine that placed one God above nature removed the restraints placed on primitive man by his belief that the environment itself was divine. Monotheistic man's impulses were no longer restrained by a pious worship of nature, and the God of Genesis told man to subdue and master the earth, proclaiming man's dominion over the natural world.[1] This approach is baseless, however: in both content and spirit the Jewish tradition negates the arrogant proposal that the earth is man's unqualified dominion.

In presenting a Jewish theology of the environment, I draw on three types of sources: *halakhah, aggadah,* and *tefillah. Halakhah,* from the verb meaning "to go," refers figuratively to the rules and statutes by which one is guided. It includes not only the Jewish scriptures, but also their traditional interpretation in the literature of the "Oral Law"—the Mishnah, Talmud, commentaries, codes, and responsa.[2] *Aggadah,* from the verb meaning "to tell," describes the vast nonjuristic literature, including biblical exegesis, homilies, parables, and proverbs, whose aim is religious and moral instruction and edification.[3] Finally, *tefillah* is prayer or liturgy. In his seminal work on Judaism in the early Christian era, George Foote Moore observed that "the true nature of a religion is most clearly revealed by what men seek from God in it. The public and private prayers of the Jews thus show not only what they esteemed the best and most satisfying goods, but their beliefs about the character of God and his relation to them, and their responsive feelings toward Him."[4] *Tefillah* also has a didactic dimension. Rooted in the halakhic and aggadic traditions, it embodies their spirit and can be a vehicle for educating the worshipper. Indeed, the verb for prayer, *hitpalel*, is in the reflexive mode, as if in praying the worshipper is also addressing himself.[5] While the first source, *halakhah*, is the obvious guide in practical issues, as *aggadah* and *tefillah* sensitize man, they too offer important guidance and direction in establishing the outlines of a Jewish theology of the environment.

In formulating such a theology, three primary questions must be addressed: To whom does the world belong? What is the plan or purpose of creation? What are the practical consequences of the answers to the above questions? Does the tradition translate the theological dimension into reality? If so, how?

The Proprietorship of the World

The argument that the Bible gave man dominion over nature and with it license to destroy at will, is based on the story of creation. Specifically, it relates to God's placing all of creation in Adam's hands with the directive to "master it" (Genesis 1:28–30). In the same narrative, however, it is apparent that man was not given a license to destroy at will (Genesis 2:15). To the contrary, God never fully relinquishes dominion over the world. In promulgating the laws of the sabbatical year (Leviticus 25:23), he reasserts his proprietorship over creation, stating, "The land is mine."

This principle of divine ownership of nature is enunciated in the *halakhah* and is the basis for several categories of liturgical blessings. According to the *Tosefta*, "Man may not taste anything until he has recited a blessing, as it is written

'The earth is the Lord's and the fullness thereof' (Psalm 24:1). Anyone who derives benefit from this world without a (prior) blessing is guilty of misappropriating sacred property."[6] The list of blessings based on this concept includes numerous specialized and general blessings recited on comestibles and a host of rules and regulations regarding their application and priorities.

For example, there are specialized blessings for bread ("Blessed art Thou, Lord our God, King of the universe, who bringest forth bread from the earth"), for fruit that grows on trees ("Blessed art Thou . . . who createst the fruit of the tree"), for fruit that grows in the soil ("Blessed art Thou . . . who createst the fruit of the earth), and for non-growing comestibles (Blessed art Thou . . . by whose words all things come into being). In addition, Jewish law prescribes various blessings upon observing or enjoying natural phenomena, for example, smelling spices, seeing the wonders of nature, seeing an electrical storm, seeing a rainbow. In all these instances man speaks not as the master of nature, but by the grace and goodness of God, as its beneficiary.[7]

The sense that man partakes in a world that is not exclusively his receives expression in an aggadic interpretation of the phrase "yumat ha-met" (Deuteronomy 17:6)—literally, "let the dead one be killed." The implied question, of course, is, How can a person be dead before he is executed? The Midrash Tanhuma explains: "An evil person is considered dead, for he sees the sun shining and does not bless 'the Creator of light' (from the morning prayer); he sees the sun setting and does not bless 'him who brings on the evening' (from the evening prayer); he eats and drinks and offers no blessings."[8] Thus, while man is placed on the earth to "master it," he does so in the Jewish tradition as a bailee, responsible and answerable to the will of his Master and obliged to acknowledge God's proprietorship at all times.

The Divine Plan

The fact that God is Creator endows all of creation with an intrinsic significance and importance. The Talmud observes: "Of all that the Holy One Blessed be He created in His world, He created nothing in vain [superfluous]."[9] Nothing in creation is useless or expendable; everything manifests some divine purpose. It follows, therefore, that there is a divine interest in maintaining the natural order of the universe.

Several expressions of this theme are to be found in conjunction with the laws of hybridization and mingling (*kilayim*). "My statutes you shall keep; you shall not let your cattle mate with a different kind, you shall not sow your field with two kinds of seed, you shall not wear a garment of wool and linen" (Leviticus 19:19). The context within which this law is recorded is of special importance—it is posed between the command to love one's neighbor and laws about forbidden conjugal relations. The laws that surround our text deal with the social order while the laws of crossbreeding deal with the natural order. From their juxtaposition it seems clear that all are part of a broader concern of the Bible to maintain the order of the world—natural and social—as created and envisioned by God.

An exegetical passage in the Palestinian Talmud epitomizes this teaching. Commenting on the opening phrase in this verse, "my statutes you shall keep," the rabbis define these statutes as "hukkot she-hakakti be-olami," "the statutes that I have legislated in my world"; that is, you may not disturb or disrupt the natural law.[10]

This theme is developed further in a thirteenth-century study of the commandments called *Sefer Ha-hinukh*. Explaining the roots of this commandment against "mingling," the author says: "the Holy One created this world with wisdom, knowledge, and understanding and formed all creatures in accordance with their needs. . . . He commanded each species to reproduce according to its kind . . . and not to have species intermingle, lest something be lacking in them and His blessings no longer apply to them."[11] Man was therefore enjoined from undermining the work of creation by engaging in acts of hybridization or intermingling. Similarly, the Sefer Ha-hinukh explains the injunction against sorcery: "Therefore we were commanded to remove from the world anyone who attempts this [sorcery], for he goes against the wishes of God who desires the settling [of the world] in the natural order that was set from creation and this [sorcerer] comes to change everything."[12]

Judaism's concern with the violation or distortion of nature is demonstrated in a Talmudic tale. A poor man's wife died in childbirth and he could not afford to hire a wet nurse. A miracle occurred and he developed breasts and suckled the child himself. Upon hearing this, Rav Yosef commented: "Come and see how great is this man that such a miracle was performed for him." To which his colleague Abaye retorted: "On the contrary, how lowly is this man that the orders of creation were changed on his account."[13] While undoubtedly sharing Rav Yosef's concern for the well-being of the infant, Abaye simply could not countenance such an unthinkable violation of the rules of nature.

Operative Principles

Judaism's genuine concern for maintaining what the rabbis called *sidrei bereshit*—the orders of creation, the plan and intent of the Creator, is expressed in several ways. Juridically we may distinguish two categories: first, injunctions against the despoliation of nature and natural resources and, second, legal imperatives regarding the development and conservation of the God-given environment.

Despoliation

Bal tashhit. The Bible (Deuteronomy 20:19) forbids the destruction of trees by an army besieging an enemy city. In the *halakhah* this biblical injunction—known as *bal tashhit* (you shall not wantonly destroy)—has been expanded to form a protective legal umbrella encompassing almost the entire realm of ecological concerns. These extensions affect three aspects of the law of *bal tashhit:* the situation, the object, and the method of destruction.[14]

While literally the Bible applies *bal tashhit* only to military tactics, the commentaries observe that the choice of this situation was not intended to limit its applicability; the Bible simply cited the most likely situation in which such destruction might occur.[15] The Talmud applies *bal tashhit* to numerous nonmilitary situations. Maimonides, in his eleventh-century code, declares: "This penalty [flogging, the punishment imposed for violating this biblical rule] is imposed not only for cutting it down during a siege; whenever a fruit-yielding tree is cut down with destructive intent, flogging is incurred."[16]

The *halakhah* extends the compass of *bal tashhit* with regard to the object destroyed, as well. Not only trees but "all things" are included by the Talmud under this rubric.[17] Specifically, the Talmud mentions the destruction of food, clothing, furniture, and even water as being in violation of *bal tashhit.*[18] The nineteenth-century code of Shneour Zalman of Ladi sums up the consensus of Jewish legal opinion, when he rules that "the spoiler of all objects from which man may benefit violates this negative commandment [*bal tashhit*]."[19] Similarly, the *halakhah* extends the jurisdiction of *bal tashhit* to include indirect and partial destruction as violations of this principle.[20]

The ethical implications of this analysis are clear. Man bears the responsibility for the destruction—complete or incomplete, direct or indirect—of all objects that may be of potential benefit or use to mankind. As part of the divine plan of creation himself, man has the obligation to respect his inanimate and animate counterparts in the world.

Endangered species. Jewish tradition also addresses itself to the problem of the endangered species. An *aggadah* in the Talmud recreates the scene from the ark and has the raven rebuke Noah, saying: "You must hate me, for you did not choose [to send a scout] from the species of which there are seven (that is, the clean birds of which Noah was commanded to take seven pairs), but from a species of which there are only two. If the power of the sun or the power of the cold overwhelm me, would not the world be lacking a species?"[21] This concern over the destruction of a species is also invoked by the medieval commentator Nahmanides to explain the biblical injunction against slaughtering a cow and her calf on the same day (Leviticus 22:28) and the taking of a bird with her young (Deuteronomy 22:6). "Scripture will not permit a destructive act that will cause the extinction of a species, even though it has permitted the ritual slaughtering of that species (for food). And he who kills mother and sons in one day, or takes them while they are free to fly away, is considered as if he destroyed that species."[22] The *Sefer Ha-hinukh* offers a similar explanation, stating that there is divine providence for each species and that God desires them to be perpetuated.[23]

This theoretical sensitivity for animal life is translated into popular custom in a most touching manner. According to custom, a person wearing new attire is blessed: "May they wear out and may they be renewed (that is, may you get new ones)." According to some authorities, this is not to be recited in the case of shoes or other garments made from animal skins since, by implication, it calls for the killing of yet another animal.[24]

Maintenance and Development of the Environment

Thus far, we have seen how Jewish tradition views the environment as God's domain and enjoins man from upsetting the *sidrei bereshit* (order of creation). There exists another dimension to man's relationship to the universe: his role as creator, as extender of *sidrei bereshit.*

Several ordinances regulating Jewish life in ancient Israel offer further guidance to our study and introduce a principle of fundamental importance to our topic: *yishuv ha-aretz* ("the settling of the land"). The Mishnah states: "One may not raise goats or sheep in the land of Israel," because by grazing they defoliate property and thereby interfere with the process of *yishuv ha-aretz.*[25] The same legal principle is invoked by the Mishnah in ruling that "all trees are suited for piling on the altar except for the vine and olive tree."[26] Since these trees represented the principal products of Israel, the rabbis feared that permitting their use on the altar might lead to the decimation of the groves and vineyards and irreparably damage the Holy Land.[27] The operative principle in these two cases, *yishuv ha-aretz,* calls upon the Jew in his homeland to balance the economic, environmental, and even religious needs of society carefully to assure the proper development and settling of the land.[28] In its active mode it demands that specific actions be taken to promote the maintenance and conservation of the natural environment.

The Jewish Scriptures mandate the establishment of a *migrash,* an open space one thousand cubits wide around the Levitical cities, to be maintained free of all construction and cultivation.[29] According to Maimonides, this applied to all cities in Israel.[30] The reason, as explained by the eleventh-century commentator Rashi, is that the open space is an amenity to the city.[31] The need for such a provision is ultimately based upon the principle of *yishuv ha-aretz.*[32] The implication in this and in other such cases is that *yishuv ha-*

aretz requires man to consider the consequences of his creative activities in the world, not merely to clear stones and build cities or to avoid acts of wanton destruction but to maintain a proper balance in the environment, providing the necessary amenities while insuring the mutual security of society and nature.

A striking example of this principle in action may be found in the fourteenth-century code of Jacob ben Asher, known as the *Tur*. In discussing the "rights of preemption" that a farmer has in his neighbor's property, the *Tur* notes that these rights are suspended if the purchaser acquired the land for the purpose of building a house and the owner of the adjacent field wants the land for sowing, since there is a greater *yishuv ha-olam* (settlement of the world) accomplished by building houses than by sowing. However, if the neighbor wishes to plant trees, he can remove the purchaser, since trees are more important for *yishuv ha-olam* than houses.[33]

An important change has been made in this last case. In explaining the law the *Tur* employs the term *yishuv ha-olam* (settlement of the world) instead of *yishuv ha-aretz* (settling the land of Israel), thereby extending the concept and its legal application beyond the borders of the land of Israel.[34] Nor is Rabbi Jacob ben Asher the only authority to do so. For example, the eighteenth-century scholar Rabbi Jacob Emden applied the concept of *yishuv ha-aretz* to a situation arising in Germany, concluding that even in cases where a destructive act is for sacred purposes and therefore not in violation of *bal tashhit*, considerations of *yishuv ha-aretz*, man's obligation to equitably and ethically continue the process of "settling the world," may render it illegal.[35]

The aforementioned cases are a far cry from the carte blanche desired by some environmentalists in their struggle to protect our natural resources. They do not offer unquestioning protection to the natural environment; nor do they

47

offer an immutable schedule of priorities to guide the actions of man. They do, however, enunciate an important legal and moral principle: the environment, like man, has certain unalienable rights, and these rights are endowed to it by the Creator—and, as a result, they may not be summarily dismissed or violated. It is the obligation of society to respect and protect these rights with the same procedures, institutions, and legislative initiatives that are employed to guarantee and protect the rights of man. And even if it, at times, must be done (as in the case of the *Tur*) at the expense of personal privileges and individual rights.

Conclusion

While nature has indeed been, to use Weber's term, "disenchanted" by the biblical creation epic, it is wrong to conclude that by releasing man from primitive constraints monotheism has given him license or incentive to destroy. In the Jewish tradition nature may be disenchanted, but never "despiritualized." For Judaism nature serves as a guide and inspiration. "Bless the Lord, O my soul," cries out the Psalmist as he views the heaven and earth and the wonders of creation. "How great are Thy works, O Lord; in wisdom You have made them all; the earth is full of your possessions" (Psalm 104:1, 24). Even a cursory glance at the daily prayer book reveals the depth to which the Jew must be stirred by nature and recognize in it a profound manifestation of God. The legal and ethical imperatives to preserve and conserve the environment are highlighted as the daily liturgy begins with a blessing for the rooster who distinguishes between day and night. The following blessings and Psalms to God as Creator offer in nature a spiritual sustenance for man's faith.[36]

Similarly, the pilgrimage festivals ordained by the Bible do not just celebrate historic events but mark the agricultural cycle—spring, first fruits, harvest—even for the child who has never seen an orchard or walked in a field of grain. The prayers for dew and rain recited on Passover and Tabernacles respectively alert man to the needs of nature and to his own dependence on the vagaries of rain, wind, and sun.

Thus, even in the midst of the concrete urban setting, prayer and ritual keep man in touch with nature, teach him to revere nature, and heighten his sense of dependence on nature. Suffused with the spirit of the Psalms, he comes to view nature as a living testimony to a living God. Says the Talmud: "He who goes out in the spring and views the trees in bloom must recite, "Blessed is He who left nothing lacking in His world and created beautiful creatures and beautiful trees for mankind to glorify in."[37] Praying man admires, praises, and is inspired by nature; how can he wantonly destroy it?

The Talmud tells the story of a farmer who was clearing stones from his field and throwing them onto a public thoroughfare. A *hasid* (pious man) rebuked him, saying, "Worthless one! Why are you clearing stones from land which is *not* yours and depositing them on property which *is* yours?" The farmer scoffed at him for this strange reversal of the facts. In the course of time the farmer had to sell his field, and as he was walking on the public road, he fell on those same stones he had thoughtlessly deposited there. He then understood the truth of the *hasid*'s words: the damage he had wrought in the public domain was ultimately damage to his own property and well-being.[38]

Modern man, like the ancient farmer of our parable, suffers from self-inflicted wounds. The reason for his suffering is perhaps best analyzed by the rabbis in the following passage from *Ethics of the Fathers* (a tractate of the Mishnah). "Ha-kin'ah ve-ha-ta'avah ve-ha-kavod motzi'in et ha-adam min ha-olam."[39] Jealousy, desire, and pursuit of glory remove man from this world. Or, in the modern idiom, keeping up with the Joneses, impulse control breakdown, and ego tripping—these are at the root of man's estrangement from nature. In this aphorism and in countless other sources, Judaism calls upon man to control his appetites and respect the rights of others. In the final analysis, this is perhaps the key to all of conservation ethics.

Notes

1. Arnold Toynbee, "The Genesis of Pollution," *New York Times*, 16 September 1973, sec. 4. This essay was based on an article that appeared in *Horizon Magazine* at that time.
2. For an excellent sketch of the literature of the *halakhah*, see David M. Feldman, *Marital Relations, Birth Control, and Abortion in Jewish Law* (New York: Schocken Books, 1974), pp. 3–18.
3. George Foote Moore, *Judaism in the First Centuries of the Christian Era* (New York: Schocken Books, 1971), 1:161–63.
4. Ibid., 2:212.
5. Rabbi Samson Raphael Hirsch in his commentary to Psalms 5:3 and 32:6 emphasizes that the process of prayer entails self-cognition on the part of the worshipper.
6. *Tosefta, Berakhot*, 4:1.
7. Philip Birnbaum, ed., *Daily Prayer Book* (New York: Hebrew Publishers, 1977), pp. 773–75.
8. *Tanhuma, Berakha*, sec. 7. This theme is particularly stressed in the liturgy for New Year's Day, which, according to tradition, is not only the Day of Judgment, but also the anniversary of creation.
9. *Shabbat*, 77b.
10. *Kilayim*, 1:7. Cf. the tana'itic midrash to Leviticus, *Sifra*.
11. *Sefer Ha-hinukh*, no. 244. Maimonides, recognizing the source of this law in the "natural order," rules that this prohibition applies to gentiles as well in the cases of grafting and interbreeding. "Laws of Kings," *Mishneh Torah*, 10:6.

12. *Sefer Ha-hinukh*, no. 62.

13. *Shabbat*, 53b.

14. For a detailed discussion of these laws, see *"Bal tashhit,"* Encyclopedia Talmudit (Jerusalem, 1963), 3:335–37. Also see Jonathan I. Helfand, "Ecology and the Jewish Tradition," *Judaism* 20 (1971): 331–33.

15. See, for example, the commentary *Da'at Zekenim mi-ba'alei Ha-tosefot* to Deuteronomy 20:19.

16. "Laws of Kings," *Mishneh Torah* 6:8. See also the *Kesef Mishneh* (commentary to Maimonides' code): *Sefer Mitzvot Godol* [=*SeMaG*], negative commandment no. 229; and Rabbi David Kimhi's commentary to 2 Kings 3:19.

17. *Bava Kama*, 91b. Some commentaries, however, interpret it as meaning "all *trees.*"

18. *Shabbit*, 140b; *Kiddushin*, 32a; *Shabbit*, 129a; *Yevamot*, 11b. In the latter case the text reads: "A man should not pour the water out of his cistern while others may require it." The *SeMaG* interprets this as being based on the law of *bal tashhit*. On the question of the pollution of water resources, see Nahum Rackover, "Protection of the Environment in Hebrew Sources" [in Hebrew], *Dine Yisrael* 4 (1973): 18–19.

19. "Hilkhot Shmirat ha-guf ve-nefesh," *Shulhan Arukh Ha-rav,* par. 14.

20. The *Sifri* (a tana'itic midrash) to Deut. 20:19 includes the cutting off of water supplies to trees as a violation of the rule. See also Maimonides, "Law of Kings," *Mishneh Torah* 6:8. Incomplete destruction is cited by the Talmud in *Kiddushin*, 32a (see Rashi) and *Bava Kama*, 91b.

21. *Sanhedrin* 108b.

22. Nahmanides, commentary to Deuteronomy 22:6. See also his comments in Leviticus 19:19 on the laws of *kilayim:* "He who mixes kinds denies and confounds the act of creation." These comments contrast with and undoubtedly modify his strong statements in Genesis 1:26, 28 regarding man's mastery over creation.

23. *Sefer Ha-hinukh*, nos. 294, 545.

24. *Shulhan Arukh, Orah Hayyim*, 233:6. On the Jewish attitude toward hunting and killing for sport, see Sidney B. Hoenig,

"The Sport of Hunting: A Humane Game?" *Tradition* 11, no. 3 (1970): 13–21.

25. *Bava Kama,* 79b and Rashi.
26. *Mishnah Tamid,* 2:3.
27. *Tamid,* 29b; Maimonides, "Laws of Things Banned from the Altar," *Mishneh Torah,* 7:3.
28. This principle is also invoked in numerous other instances. For a review of this literature, see the *Encyclopedia Talmudit* (Jerusalem, 1956), 2:225–26.
29. Numbers 35:2–5.
30. "Laws of Sabbatical and Jubilee Years," *Mishneh Torah,* 13:5.
31. See the commentary of Rashi to Numbers 35:2 and to *Arakhin,* 33b.
32. *Encyclopedia Talmudit,* 2:226.
33. *Tur Hosen Mishpat,* par. 175 (based on *Bava Metzi'ah,* folio 108b).
34. Ibid. See Bet Yosef (commentary of Rabbi Joseph Karo), no. 43, and the comments of *Prishah* to this paragraph in the *Tur.*
35. *She'ilat Ya'avetz,* pt. 1, responsum 76.
36. Birnbaum, *Daily Prayer Book,* pp. 15, 51ff.
37. *Berakhot,* 43a.
38. *Tosefta, Bava Kama,* 10:2. Cf. *Bava Kama,* 50b.
39. *Pirke Avot,* 4:21.

Susan Power Bratton

Christian Ecotheology and the Old Testament

The role of Judeo-Christian theology in developing environmental ethics has often been portrayed as negative or inadequate to modern problems. Historians like Lynn White, Jr., and Roderick Nash have blamed either the church or biblical writings for encouraging abuse of nature.[1] Even modern theologians from the Christian tradition, such as John B. Cobb, Jr., find the traditional Judeo-Christian view inadequate and have suggested we must seek new theological or philosophical alternatives.[2] The question is a complex one, however, because the Western church has, through the centuries, neglected the study of creation.[3] Interest in creation theology has been minor compared to other doctrinal issues such as soteriology and Christology, and many Christian scholars have a better understanding of the Greek texts than of the older Hebrew writings. The attitude of the church may, therefore, not have been based on a thorough analysis of Scripture. Further, the recognition of a global environmental crisis is a recent phenomenon; our current scientific understanding of the processes of environmental change was not available at the time the Scriptures were written.

One possible way to develop a sound Christian ecotheology, and to determine a proper Christian approach to

environmental ethics, is first to analyze scriptural texts concerning God-creation and man-creation relationships. We
can then draw an accurate picture of what the Biblical writers originally meant when discussing creation. My purpose
in this paper is to look at the works of modern Old Testament scholars, particularly Walther Eichrodt, Gerhard von
Rad, and Claus Westermann, who have made substantial
contributions to our current understanding of Hebrew theology, including theology of creation. I begin with an overview of important components of Old Testament thinking
on both creation and God as Creator, and discuss these ideas
in relation to the development of a viable Christian ecotheology.

It should be pointed out at the beginning that modern Old
Testament critics are not in agreement regarding the best
methodology for analysis; nor do they all handle the question of the historical content of the texts in the same way.
Some critics treat the Old Testament as if it has one central
theme; others see it as presenting several themes. Some authors , such as Gerhard von Rad and Brevard Childs, attempt
to include the entire canon in their work, or at least hold
that all the books must be considered, while others, such as
Claus Westermann, do not see all the books as equally
important or interpretable in terms of central themes. (Westermann omits the wisdom literature from consideration in
developing Old Testament theology.) Writers also differ
greatly in how they relate the Old Testament to the New
Testament: some disregard the New Testament entirely;
others attempt to integrate the two sets of works, even
though they are the products of different historical and cultural environments and were composed in different languages.[4] Although these disagreements among scholars are
important to the detailed study of the Old Testament, they
are generally beyond the scope of this paper. I attempt to
avoid these conflicts by using the principles for Old Testa-

ment theology outlined by Hasel.[5] These are (in edited form):

(1) Biblical theology is to be treated as a historical-theological discipline,[6] and (2) the method must be historical and theological from the starting point.[7] These are quite different from many attempts at constructing ecotheologies or at evaluating the potential success of a Judeo-Christian ecotheology, in that most such efforts are either historical or theological, but not both.

(3) The only appropriate source for Old Testament theology is the Old Testament, not related literatures and traditions.[8] This principle is important to ecotheologies where authors have seen passages such as the Genesis accounts only as versions of myths derived from other sources. Hasel would reject this treatment as inadequate.

(4) An analysis need not follow the order of books in the canon, but should be based, as best can be determined, on the dates of the writings.[9]

(5) "An OT [Old Testament] theology not only seeks to know the theology of the various books, or groups of writings; it also attempts to draw together and present the major themes of the OT. . . . OT theology must allow its themes, motifs, and concepts to be formed for it by the OT itself."[10] We must, therefore, be careful not to do what many environmental writers have done and see the Old Testament largely from the point of view of our own current philosophical interests and cultural environment. If we are to evaluate Old Testament thought, we must do this with a recognition both of the writers' original intentions and of the Hebrew worldview. Old Testament theology must be based on what the Old Testament itself actually says about something. Further, we must discriminate between those concepts, events, or practices merely recorded or described in the texts and those which are affirmed or condoned. Since any discussion of creation theology must attempt to be eclectic, care must be

taken not to replace the priorities of the ancient Hebrews with our own.

(6) "As the OT is interrogated for its theology, it answers first of all by yielding various theologies, namely those of the individual books and groups of writings, and then by yielding the theologies of various longitudinal themes. But the name of our discipline as theology of the OT is not only concerned to present and explicate the variety of different theologies. The concept foreshadowed by the name of the discipline has one theology in view, namely the theology of the OT."[11] For our purposes, this implies that in analyzing creation theology of the Old Testament, one has to look both at individual books and at the overall presentation of all the books. In light of Hasel's remarks, creation theology might be better termed the "creation theme" and seen as one of many theological strands, intimately connected to the other themes that combine to make Old Testament theology. In pursuing the creation theme one cannot depend solely on the first few chapters of Genesis, nor can one ignore the wisdom literature. Many writers who have tackled the question of the adequacy of Judeo-Christian environmental ethics have relied on one or two passages of Scripture and may thus have misunderstood the total thrust of the scriptural texts.[12]

(7) "The name 'theology of the Old Testament' implies the larger context of the Bible of which the New Testament is the other part. An integral OT theology must demonstrate its basic relationship to the NT or to NT theology."[13] This is, of course, critical in determining how the Old Testament should relate to Christian ecotheology.

Within this theological framework then, I attempt to develop an overview of the creation theology of the Old Testament, and try to avoid both excessive cultural distortion of the Old Testament's meaning and incomplete analysis of the Hebrew position.

The Creator God

Although many environmental commentators begin the discussion of Judeo-Christian ecotheology with the question of man's dominion, most Old Testament commentators begin the discussion of creation theology with an investigation of God as creator. The modern reader tends to look for passages explaining man's relationship to nature, but this is of itself a poor way to start analyzing Old Testament texts, which are very theocentric. Westermann, for example, states: "A theology of the Old Testament has the task of summarizing and viewing together what the Old Testament as a whole, in all its sections, says about God."[14]

In order to answer our first question—How does the Old Testament present God as acting in the original creation?—we can begin by comparing the Hebrew presentation to those of neighboring cultures. The Old Testament has some striking parallels to Babylonian creation accounts[15] and was, of course, developed in an environment where there was considerable threat of syncretism with Canaanite and Egyptian cultures. Despite some borrowing of imagery, the Hebrew picture of God as Creator was quite distinct. In the Babylonian accounts, the god Marduk fights chaos and in the process creates life and order. In the Genesis accounts chaos is mentioned but is conceptually different. The "Enuma Elish" epic of the Babylonians describes a watery chaos that is not only living matter, but is part of the first two principles, *apsu* and *tiamat*, "in whom all elements of the future universe were comingled."[16] Thus, in the Babylonian epic the universe is preexisting. In Genesis, God creates all matter and imparts life to his creatures via his divine breath.[17] The gods of the Babylonians arise out of the primeval chaos and are, therefore, merely deified natural forces. In the Hebrew accounts, even when Yahweh confronts chaos, "creation does not draw the deity into the flux of the world process,"[18] much less generate God or the godly. The Old Testament presents the universe as a creation of God, which he transcends. This is in marked contrast to both Babylonian and Canaanite religions, where heavenly bodies, trees, and other natural objects were credited with supernatural power and thereby deified.

From the very beginning Yahweh is seen as acting spiritually and personally to create order. In the Genesis account and in the prophets, Yahweh creates through his word. These accounts provide us "with an idea of the absolute effortlessness of the divine creative action" and also make clear that "if the world is the product of the creative word, it is therefore . . . sharply separated in nature from God himself—it is neither an emanation nor a mythically understood manifestation of the divine nature and power."[19] This has a number of implications for the relationship between God and creation. As Langdon Gilkey observes, no part of creation shares "divinity in any of its aspects, as if the being or substance of God had separated itself into many pieces to become the being of each creature."[20] Furthermore, the difference between God and his creation "is the result of God's creative act, not of a 'fall' or turning away from God" and God's transcendence is itself a source of the "alienation" of creation from God.[21]

The spirit, or in Hebrew *ruah* (breath of God), is instrumental in the original creative act, and is held throughout the Old Testament to be the very principle of life. Both man and animals come to life through this breath of God. If God withdraws his spirit, then "every creature must sink down in death."[22] It should be noted that this spirit is also seen as "the instrument of God in salvation history,"[23] "the consumating power of the new age,"[24] and "the power behind the life of the people of God."[25] Neither the spirit nor the creation event are independent of other major Old Testament themes. As Claus Westermann points out: "Only he who is active in everything could be savior. Since God is One, the savior must also be the creator. It follows that in the Old Testament the history established by God's saving deed was expanded to include the beginning of everything that happens. The savior of Israel is the creator; the creator is the savior of Israel. What began in creation issues into Israel's history."[26]

Environmental commentators who restrict their reading to Genesis often miss the complex interweaving of the Old Testament concept of creation with other themes. Von Rad even proposes "that Israel was interested in creation not because of nature and its problems, but because of history."[27] The "history only" point of view is extreme, but a careful reading of the entire Old Testament shows creation as relating to history, salvation, the people of Israel, wisdom, and eschatological events. The references are scattered throughout the Old Testament , but are most numerous in Psalms, the Prophets, and the wisdom literature.

In the middle section of the book of Isaiah[28] (chapters 40–55), for example, the author combines two major Hebrew traditions, that of God the Creator and of Yahweh of the Exodus as God active in history. As von Rad suggests: "A special feature in Deutero-Isaiah's thought about creation is, of course, that he does not regard creation as a work by itself, something additional to Yahweh's historical acts. . . . For him creation is the first of Yahweh's miraculous historical acts and a remarkable witness to his will to save. The conclusive evidence for this 'soteriological' conception of creation is the fact that Deutero-Isaiah can at one time speak of Yahweh, the creator of the world and at another of Yahweh, the creator of Israel."[29]

In Isaiah 40–55, the original act of creation and the creation of the people of Israel through the Exodus become types for a "new saving event" and thus are integrated into eschatology. Yahweh can, through the power of his word and his spirit, create a new kingdom of Israel. Deutero-Isaiah makes frequent use of the word *bara,* which is also used in the first chapters of Genesis to imply a creative act, such as the creation of Adam, which only God can perform. *Bara* is used not only to refer to the first creation, but also in establishing God's loving kindness toward Israel. Since both the original creation and the new saving event are accomplished by the Word and the Spirit of God, these deeds of creation are "personal, responsible" acts of God.[30]

Having established that God the Creator is transcendent and that his creative acts include not only the creation of the universe via his word, but also the creation and salvation of his people, we now can ask, what are the characteristics, according to the Old Testament, of creation itself? Returning to the Genesis account, we find that after the earth is separated from the seas "God saw that it was good" [31] and that at the very end of the creation effort, "God saw everything that he had made, and behold, it was very good."[32] The English translation misses the full meaning of the Hebraic adjective *tob,* which can mean "good" and "beautiful": "In the concluding sentence the listener can thus also hear the echo: 'Behold, it was very beautiful.' The beauty of creation has its foundation in the will of the creator; beauty belongs to God's works. Whoever speaks about the work of the creator also speaks about what is beautiful."[33] The creation accounts include a judgment by God, and it is a highly favorable one.

A second characteristic of creation is that it is blessed by God. When God said, "Be fruitful and multiply," he gave a blessing that continues outside of the events of salvation history.[34] Although many environmental critiques mention this statement only in regard to humankind or actually treat the statement as if it were a curse, the original intent was both universal and beneficial.

A third characteristic of creation is that it praises or glorifies God. In Psalm 148:3–10, for example, all creation is called on to praise God:

> Praise him, sun and moon,
>> praise him, all you shining stars!
> Praise him you highest heavens,
>> and you waters above the heavens!
> . . . .
> Praise the Lord from the earth,
>> you sea monsters and all deeps,
> fire, hail, snow and frost,
>> stormy wind fulfilling his command!
>
> Mountains and all hills,
>> fruit trees and all cedars!
> Beasts and all cattle,
>> creeping things and flying birds!

The same type of imagery is found in other books such as Job and Isaiah. Isaiah 55:12 reads:

> For you shall go out in joy,
>> and be led forth in peace;
> the mountains and the hills before you
>> shall break forth into singing,
> and all the trees of the field shall
>> clap their hands.

Creation may also act as a party in a covenant lawsuit concerning the sins of the people of Israel, as in Micah 6:1–2:

> Hear what the Lord says:
> Arise, plead your case before the mountains
> and let the hills hear your voice.
> Hear, you mountains, the controversy of the Lord,
> and you enduring foundations of the earth;
> for the Lord has a controversy with his people;
> and he will contend with Israel.

All this implies that God has a continuing concern for creation and that creation is continually able to respond to God. Further, in Deutero-Isaiah, creation is described as participating in the new saving event.

It should be noted that the Old Testament usually deals with creation in its entirety and there is no divine hierarchy within the whole. All is good and beautiful, while none is in any way God. For the ancient Hebrew, evil is not a necessary element in creation, and the evil now operating on and through creation will ultimately be defeated by the "new saving event" which will also be a new creative act.

Adam in Creation

Having looked at the role of God, we now need to analyze how humankind relates to God in the midst of creation, and thereby relates to creation. The first problem concerns the statement in Genesis 1:26: "Then God said: 'Let us make man in our image, after our likeness.'" This has been interpreted by some authors as simply setting man above creation, but it might be better interpreted as setting man in an especially close relationship to God. Von Rad states in his commentary on the passage that "God participates more intimately and intensively in this than in the earlier works of creation."[35] Westermann goes further and suggests that "this is not primarily a statement about human life, but about the creation of human life by God. The creature God is now planning is to stand in relationship to him; humans are to correspond to God so that something can happen between them and God, so that God can speak to them and they can answer."[36]

In the same verse, immediately after God declares that Adam is to be made in the divine image, we find the controversial passage: "And let them have dominion over the fish of the sea, and over the birds of the air, and over cattle, and over all the earth and over every creeping thing that creeps upon the earth." Many environmental commentators have taken this as a presentation of earth to human beings as a gift to them, when in reality it is a more complex matter of setting man to work under the continuing authority of God. Even the creation in the image of God is not a gift or a declaration of simple superiority but a necessity required before Adam can rule. As Von Rad suggests:

> This commission to rule is not considered as belonging to the definition of God's image; but is its consequence, i.e., that for which man is capable because of it. . . . Just as powerful earthly kings, to indicate their claim to dominion, erect an image of themselves in the provinces of their empire where they do not personally appear, so man is placed upon earth in God's image as God's sovereign emblem. He is really only God's representative, summoned to maintain and enforce God's claim to dominion over the earth.[37]

Eichrodt basically concurs when he writes:

> The connection between Man's creation in the image of God and his dominant position within the world of creatures is . . . indeed associated with the declaration of God's intention to create Man, being mentioned as a consequence of the especially close relationship of this creature to his Creator; but in the detailed exposition of the divine plan it is then quite clearly distinguished from this relationship as a separate item which has to be promised by a special creative act of blessing. Subjugation of the earth and dominion over its creatures bestows on the human race a common universal task, and in the execution of this task Man's special nature is to become visibly effective in that he is hereby made the responsible representative of the divine cosmic Lord.[38]

The command to take dominion was necessary for man to assume his special responsibility. That is, the command was both enabling and differentiating. Man's dominion was not a simple transfer of civil power but actually a spiritual transfer of authority centered in a special creative act.

After giving man dominion, God repeats the blessing given to the creatures and applies it to humankind: "And God blessed them, and God said multiply, and fill the earth and subdue it; and have dominion over the fish of the sea and over the birds of the air and over every living thing that moves upon the earth."[39] Again, environmental commentators have tended to emphasize the dominion aspect and have neglected the fact that God gives mankind exactly the same blessing as the rest of creation and that he requires that man assume the responsibility of representing God's interests. As Westermann states:

> These verses sum up what it means to be a human being; man is what he is precisely as a creature of God; his creature-state determines his capability and the meaning of his existence.
> What man is capable of is bestowed on him by the blessing. The blessing seen as controlling the power of fertility is a gift which man shares with the animals. It is something that binds man and beasts together.[40]

Thus, we have in this short text, man set in the image of God and therefore in special relationship to him. Man is set above creation, but because he is given the same blessing as creation, he is therefore insured of creatureliness.

In Genesis 2, which scholars hold to be a second separate creation account combined with Genesis 1, "The Lord God took the man and put him in the garden of Eden to till it and keep it."[41] This passage does not give a portrait of man called to be despot, but presents man as called to serve. The verb *abad*, translated as "to till," has the connotation not only of work but of service, and can be translated as "to serve" or "to be a slave to." The word *shamar* "to keep" might also be translated "to watch" or "to preserve."[42] It is important that God's power placed man in Eden to serve and preserve the earth. God then allowed man to eat the fruits of the garden. Nowhere is it implied man has a right to do this, or that the earth is man's servant to be done with as he pleases.

Some authors have pointed out that the command "to take dominion" uses the Hebrew words *rada* and *kabas*, which are very strong and imply treading down or trampling.[43] All relevant texts need to be interpreted in a compatible fashion, however, and in this context some form of ravishing the earth is clearly not intended in Genesis 2:15. James Barr has suggested that nothing more is to be read into the Hebrew words of the dominion passage than "the basic needs of settlement and agriculture," including tilling the ground, and this interpretation is satisfactorily within the limits imposed by the passage on the keeping of Eden.[44]

Following Adam's placement in Eden comes the temptation and spread of sin in Genesis 3. Man, having been given a special relationship to God and a position of power over creation, breaks his relationship with God, who then reacts to the "increasingly grave violation of his order."[45] Adam's power is limited, and these limitations affect his ability to understand and know God. Adam also ceases to comprehend godly matters, such as executing dominion and receiving the blessings of Genesis 2.[46]

In the course of rebuking Adam and Eve for the transgression in Eden, God pronounces his punishment via a curse, which includes a curse of the ground. This curse puts a stumbling block in front of Adam who is still under the commission to work given in Genesis 2:15. Henceforth, "man's work is always in some way tied up with toil and effort; every area of work throws up its thorns and thistles which can not be avoided."[47] In basic recognition that what man needs must come from creation, the passage declares that the barriers to man successfully completing his tasks are found in his broken relationship with creation itself. Although theologians disagree as to whether all creation fell with Adam, nature is, at the very least, an innocent victim, under a curse because of man's sin, and does not now fully produce its full fruits because of it.[48] From this it can be inferred that proper dominion is not an easy matter for man, who is struggling, because of the effects of sin, to relate not only to God, but also to other humans and all of nature. The breaking of the relationship with God and the expulsion from the garden also imply that dominion, as God intended it, can only be carried out with careful attention to the will of God and a tremendous effort. If dominion originally required God as both a lord and cooperator, God becomes even more necessary after the curse, because only God can lift it.

It should be recognized that much of the remainder of the Old Testament deals directly with the character of God, man's relationship to God, and other issues relevant to God's expectations of man. The establishment of covenant relationships, such as those made with Abraham or with Moses, present man with an opportunity to reestablish open communication with Yahweh. In the process of describing the expected man-God relationships the Prophets, for example, used a theology that included God as Creator. Creation had "opened up the dimension of history and saving history" for Israel and therefore is repeatedly mentioned in her sacred texts.[49]

One last series of passages deserve analysis in regard to man's relationship to nature, and these are the references to creation and wisdom in the wisdom literature. This literature is relatively late and is the beginning of an attempt to seek out the mysteries of nature. It presents wisdom as pre-existing before the rest of creation and as immanent in the world. God gave an order to his works at the very beginning, and this order is separate from the activities of men. Unlike the modern who considers wisdom and knowledge to be solely the product of human endeavor, the scholars who wrote the wisdom literature considered wisdom something created by God which existed in creation, whether man was there or not. This literature also held that the way to wisdom was through fear (not literally fear; perhaps respect or awe is a better term) of Yahweh. If someone cares to pursue it, therefore, wisdom, the key not only to order in the universe, but also the key to correct behavior or proper action before God, is available.[50] A characteristic of the wisdom literature is "the determined effort to relate the phenomenon of the world, of 'nature' with its secrets of creation, to the saving revelation addressed to man."[51] These concerns are rarely discussed in the environmental literature; yet they represent an extensive block of "how to" texts which have parallels in other religions, including those of the Far East.

God's Continuing Interaction with Creation

Rather than stop with the Genesis accounts, we can now pose the question: does God continue to interact in creation and if so, how? Since there are relatively few direct references to creation in the New Testament and the references in the Old Testament are scattered, it is easy to concentrate on the Genesis passages and to begin to take a deist view, that is, to see God as Creator only at the beginning of time. In the Old Testament God continues as Creator throughout.

As mentioned previously, God acts in creation by both blessing and saving. Blessing is different from saving in that the continuing blessing of God "is a quiet, continuous, flowing, and unnoticed working . . . which can not be captured in moments or dates. . . . Evening and morning songs speak about the activity of a blessing God."[52] In addition, God also saves individuals and communities and will ultimately redeem creation as a whole. "The entire Old Testament thus speaks of God's continuous action in addition to the acts which occur once in his saving and judging deeds."[53]

Heschel makes the point that "the fundamental thought in the Bible is not creation, but God's care for his creation."[54] On one hand, we have what modern theologians call providence: the very ordering of nature is "a revelation of God's goodness, particularly his mercy and long suffering,"[55] and on the other hand, we have God working to bring about salvation. This includes miracles (or in Old Testament terms, God's mighty deeds) which may be regarded as creative acts. The Exodus, for example, was marked by a series of miraculous events, each of which may be viewed independently as a move of God the Creator exercising his prerogatives with his handiwork. One may also see the entire Exodus, however, as a single new creative act of Yahweh.[56]

The Old Testament and Christian Ecotheology

In the preceding discussion of the Old Testament, I showed that creation theology was more to the ancient Hebrew than a theology of original creative acts; it was a theology of God's continuing interaction with both humankind and nature. The concept of an ecotheology, based on relationships between God and humankind, God and nature, and humankind and nature, therefore, has a foundation in the ancient writings and is by scriptural precedent a legitimate Christian concern.

In developing a sound Christian ecotheology, we have to accept the fact that the majority of scriptural texts directly mentioning creation are in the Old Testament, and that any dependable theology of creation must be founded on extensive Hebrew scholarship.[57] We also have to accept the fact that some common criticisms of Judeo-Christian thinking—that it does not consider God part of nature and that it sets humankind in a special position—are basically correct interpretations of Old Testament theology. Concluding that these theological attributes of Judeo-Christian thinking produce an inadequate view of nature is an oversimplification, however.

Although the Old Testament clearly and purposefully removes any trace of divinity from nature, its discussions of creation are so spiritualized that they are difficult for the modern secular reader to comprehend fully. The very fact that nature praises God gives nature continuing intrinsic value. The Old Testament stresses the spiritual and aesthetic, neither of which can be given the definite material values our modern minds would prefer. We may actually be more comfortable with the sacred groves of the Baal worshipers, because they give individual natural features a special value and avoid the problem of having to grasp the entirety of creation as the work of God remaining under his care. The holism of the Old Testament in regard to nature presents an ironic stumbling block to categorized, materialistic modern thinking.

A second area of weakness in modern Christian interpretation concerns the ideas of "man in the image of God" and of "dominion." Many people remove these from their proper spiritual context and simply assume that the earth was placed here for the benefit of humankind. This is not, however, what the texts say. What the Genesis passages and much of the rest of the Old Testament speak for is a servitude of man to God, and as a result, to God's interests. The Old Testament records many failures in this regard, and man's inability to see his responsibilities begins when Cain asks: "Am I my brother's keeper?"[58]

The themes of servitude and of covenant relationships requiring responsibility to God are woven into the entire Old Testament. In the poetic crown of the Prophets, the second half of Isaiah, we find the "suffering servant" of Yahweh, and "might see in this description of one 'despised and rejected by men' the increasingly familiar pattern . . . dominion is servitude."[59] The Old Testament also makes clear that to serve God adequately one must be faithful, diligent, self-disciplined, giving, forgiving, and so on. Dominion is not an easy task and can only be executed by continuing hard labor and overcoming major obstacles. The effort must be under God's direction and must be accomplished for God, not for personal gain.

In the United States, concepts of God and nature have had a variety of cultural associations. Barbara Novak claims that in the nineteenth century, for example, "ideas of God's nature and of God in nature became hopelessly entangled, and only the most scrupulous theologians even tried to separate them."[60] Further, Americans have often seen the natural bounty of the continent as a special blessing, and have often extended their patriotism into a perceived divine appointment as the New Jerusalem.[61] The intent of the ancient Hebrews notwithstanding, the romantic tendency to equate nature with God, on the one hand, and the conservative tendency to promote civil religion as part of the national destiny, on the other, are likely to perpetuate the confusion and misinterpretation surrounding the "dominion passage."

Since the theme of creation in the Old Testament is not independent of other themes, current Christian attitudes about creation cannot be independent of other related issues such as salvation. The attitude that "the Lord will fix it all in the end" is eschatologically correct but ignores God's continuing care and blessing via his servants. Christ's parables of the householder who returns to check on the tenants working his estate and of the king who returns to see what his servants have done with the money they have been given are good models, since God has given us both a responsibility and a blessing.

If God created the cosmos as *tob*, humankind should help to maintain it as such and preserve its aesthetic values. Unfortunately, modern English translations miss the impact of the Hebrew word, and the modern reader may secularize the passage: "And God saw that it was good for something" or "And God saw that it was full of material value." In "taking dominion" the Old Testament shows a concern both for the maintenance of the aesthetic values of creation and, in the Pentateuch and the writings of the prophets, for the just distribution of the resources available.

The Old Testament provides numerous texts on how one can serve God and the entire wisdom literature is dedicated to the topic of righteous action. The idea that the ancient writings are too weak and their view of the environment too primitive to be of much help today comes from superficial analysis or actual ignorance of the texts. The Old Testament attitude toward creation is so strongly spiritualized that it is hard for us to understand it. Moreover, the standards set on service to God are so high that most people, as the Old Testament so candidly illustrates in the case of the nation Israel, have no inclination to even try to meet them. Passages written centuries ago can be both difficult to understand and difficult to set in a meaningful modern context. It is important, however, that we avoid hasty judgments on one of the central roots of the Western spiritual heritage and that our approach to the Old Testament be both thoughtful and scholarly. Those interested in developing a Christian ecotheology should not be too cursory in their treatment of the Old Testament texts nor too glib in their assumptions concerning the will of God for creation. In-depth studies of specific writings and literatures, that is, the Psalms or the wisdom literature, and a search for more strands in the cre-

Susan Power Bratton

ation theme, will produce a better formed and sounder ecotheology and may also help to compensate for any past
Christian theological neglect of God's role as Creator.

Notes

1. Lynn White, Jr., "The Historical Roots of Our Ecological
   Crisis," *Science* 155 (1967): 1203–7; Roderick Nash, *Wilderness and the American Mind* (New Haven, Conn.: Yale University Press, 1970).
2. John B. Cobb, Jr., *Is It Too Late? A Theology of Ecology* (Beverly
   Hills, Calif.: Bruce, 1972).
3. James B. Packer, "The Gospel: Its Content and Communication," in *Down to Earth: Studies in Christianity and Culture*
   (Grand Rapids, Mich.: William B. Eerdmans, 1980), pp. 97–114.
4. Gerhard Hasel, *Old Testament Theology: Basic Issues in the
   Current Debate* (Grand Rapids, Mich.: William B. Eerdmans,
   1972).
5. Ibid., pp. 169–83.
6. Ibid., p. 169.
7. Ibid., p. 171.
8. Ibid., p. 177.
9. Ibid., p. 179.
10. Ibid., p. 180.
11. Ibid., p. 181.
12. Discussions of some of the cultural results of this sort of lim-
    ited interpretation may be found in Clarence Glacken, *Traces
    on the Rhodian Shore* (Berkeley and Los Angeles: University of
    California Press, 1967), and in Keith Thomas, *Man and the
    Natural World: A History of Modern Sensibility* (New York:
    Pantheon Books, 1983).
13. Gerhard Hasel, *Old Testament Theology*, p. 183.
14. Claus Westermann, *Elements of Old Testament Theology* (At-
    lanta: John Knox Press, 1982). Hereafter cited as Westermann,
    OTT.
15. Bernhard W. Anderson, *Creation Versus Chaos: The Rein-*

terpretation of Mythical Symbolism in the Bible (New York: Association Press, 1967).

16. Alexander Heidel, *The Babylonian Genesis* (Chicago: University of Chicago Press, 1951), p. 97.

17. Biblical scholars disagree on the question of whether the first chapter of Genesis really describes creation from nothing. Genesis 1:1 could also imply there was something present before creation, even if it was "chaos." Gerald Wilson has pointed out to me this is a semantic question, and alternate readings are possible.

18. Walther Eichrodt, *Theology of the Old Testament*, vol. 2 (Philadelphia: Westminster Press, 1967), p. 98.

19. Gerhard von Rad, *Old Testament Theology*, vol. 1 (New York: Harper and Row, 1962), p. 142 (hereafter cited as von Rad, *OTT*). This tradition is not without parallels in other cultures. The Egyptian god Ptah also creates by his word.

20. Langdon Gilkey, *Maker of Heaven and Earth* (New York : Doubleday, 1959), p. 86.

21. Ibid., p. 87.

22. Eichrodt, *Theology*, p. 48.

23. Ibid., p. 50.

24. Ibid., p. 57.

25. Ibid., p. 60.

26. Westermann, *OTT*, p. 86.

27. Gerhard von Rad, *God at Work in Israel* (Nashville: Abingdon, 1980), p. 99.

28. There is some scholarly disagreement over the number of authors of the Book of Isaiah. Conservatives hold to one author. Some critics propose three or more. The term Deutero-Isaiah is used both for chapters 40–55 and the supposed author of this section.

29. Carroll Stuhlmueller, *The Prophets and the Word of God* (Notre Dame, Ind.: Fides Publishers, 1964), p. 200.

30. Gerhard von Rad, *The Message of the Prophets* (New York: Harper and Row, 1962), p. 208.

31. Gen. 1:10; all translations are from *The New Oxford Annotated Bible* (New York: Oxford University Press, 1973).

32. Gen. 1:31.

33. Westermann, *OTT,* p. 93.
34. Gen. 1:22; Westermann, *OTT,* pp. 102–4.
35. Gerhard von Rad, *Genesis* (Philadelphia: Westminster Press, 1972), p. 57.
36. Westermann, *OTT,* p. 97.
37. Gerhard von Rad, *Genesis,* p. 57–58.
38. Eichrodt, *Theology,* p. 127.
39. Gen. 1:28.
40. Claus Westermann, *Creation* (Philadelphia: Fortress Press, 1974), p. 49.
41. Gen. 2:15.
42. Loren Wilkinson, ed., *Earth Keeping: Christian Stewardship of Natural Resources* (Grand Rapids: Eerdmans, 1980), p. 209.
43. von Rad, *Genesis,* p. 59.
44. James Barr, "Man and Nature: The Ecological Controversy and the Old Testament," in *Ecology and Religion in History,* ed. David Spring and Ellen Spring (New York: Harper and Row, 1974), pp. 63–64.
45. von Rad, *Genesis,* p. 155.
46. Claus Westermann, *Creation,* pp. 89–112.
47. Ibid., p. 102.
48. Paul Santmire, *Brother Earth: Nature God and Ecology in Time of Crisis* (New York: Thomas Nelson, 1970), pp. 163–68.
49. von Rad, *OTT,* p. 450.
50. Gerhard von Rad, *Wisdom in Israel* (Nashville: Abingdon, 1972), pp. 144–76.
51. von Rad, *OTT,* p. 449.
52. Westermann, *OTT,* p. 103.
53. Ibid.
54. Abraham Heschel, *The Prophets,* vol. 2 (New York: Harper and Row, 1962), p. 264.
55. William Dyrness, *Themes in Old Testament Theology* (Downers Grove, Ill.: Inter Varsity Press, 1979), p. 76.
56. Ibid., p. 77.
57. David Ehrenfeld justly criticized a draft of this paper for its lack of references to Jewish exegetes such as Rashi. Jewish interpretation of the Old Testament could not, of course, be based on Hasel's principles since Hasel accepts the New Testa-

ment as canonical. A thorough overview of Jewish scholarship on creation is a much-needed addition to the environmental literature and would add further depth to our understanding of the Old Testament.

58. Gen. 4:9; Wilkinson, *Earthkeeping*, p. 212.
59. Ibid., p. 214.
60. Barbara Novak, *Nature and Culture: American Landscape Painting, 1825–1875.* (New York: Oxford University Press, 1980), p. 3.
61. See, for example, Robert Linder and Richard Pierard, *Twilight of the Saints: Biblical Christianity and Civil Religion in America* (Downers Grove, Ill.: Inter Varsity Press, 1978).

Martin LaBar

A Biblical Perspective
on Nonhuman Organisms:
Values, Moral Considerability,
and Moral Agency

Beyond question, the Bible has played an enormously important role in shaping Western culture. This influence has shaped prevailing Western attitudes toward the environment to a considerable degree. Conversely, developments in Western society have changed interpretations of biblical statements relating to the environment.[1] It seems worthwhile, therefore, to examine the Bible itself to see what it says about environmental ethics. This has already been done rather thoroughly in an important area, namely, man's role,[2] although undoubtedly there is more gold to mine. In this paper, I consider not man's role, but biblical views of nature apart from man. What status does the Bible assign to nonhuman entities? Did the writers of the Bible recognize them as having intrinsic value?

There are pitfalls inherent in a topic of this type. Probably the most important one involves the diverse world view of the writers. Because of the long time span over which the Bible was written, cultural changes may have led to significant differences in world view between the authors. I sidestep this problem by supposing that cultural changes in past cultures were probably very much less rapid than they are today,[3] and, more important, that differences in world view between the writers have probably had little impact on readers. I also avoid questions about whether the Bible was divinely inspired, inerrant, and so forth, on the grounds that regardless of its status, it has been an important influence on Western thinking. We can discover what it says about nonhuman value independently of the Bible's ultimate authorship.

Two other pitfalls to avoid concern how the Bible relates to modern life. First, what has been the influence of biblical world views on our concept of nature? For example, are Western science and technology a product, direct or indirect, of our Judaeo-Christian heritage? Second, from the standpoint of those who take the Bible seriously, is there a difference between what the Bible affirms and what it depicts? In this paper, I do not discuss how, or how much, the Bible has influenced our view of nature, and I try to avoid determining what persons who take the Bible seriously should think and do about nature, based on its teachings. These pitfalls exist because they have been mined rather thoroughly by others.

The last pitfalls I am skirting are perhaps the deepest. One of them is the profound question, Did the writers of the Bible perceive nature as being of value apart from man? Another way of putting the question is to ask, Might God have created nature and not created man? The second is equally deep, and for me, equally unanswerable. Did the biblical writers believe that nature before the Fall had no negative value? It seems certain that the writers of the Bible recognized negative value after the Fall, as disease, famine, wilderness, and weather were enemies of man. Little, however, is said about life before the Fall, except perhaps that Satan and the Tree of the Knowledge of Good and Evil were present at that time. Were the consequences of the Fall positive or negative? I do not know and leave these matters for other questions about the biblical view of nonhuman nature.

For the purposes of this study, only the Old and New Testaments will be used. Without making any judgments as to the religious status of the Apocrypha, I am ignoring it because it has been much less influential than the Testaments. In what follows, I first examine the question of the value of nature in the Bible, and then turn to the issues of moral considerability and moral agency. As a guide to contemporary thinking about values, I follow in outline a recent analysis of natural value by Holmes Rolston, III.[4]

Values in Nature

Economic value. Clearly, people living in biblical times understood that there was economic value in natural entities. For instance, even such an important biblical concept as the idea of the promised land was described largely in terms of economic use (Deuteronomy 8:7–10).[5] Assuming, therefore, that the question of whether the writers of the Bible realized that natural entities can have economic value is not in doubt, I turn to the issue of whether the activity of man increases such value.

Rolston's discussion of economic value in nature is primarily from the standpoint of the effect of man's labor on nature's inherent value. He argues, moreover, that "economic value is a function of the state of science. . . ."[6] The Bible, however, was written at a time when science was nonexistent, or nearly so, depending on how science is defined. As would be expected, then, the biblical concept of economic value in nature is less dependent on technological modification of nature than economic value is today. Wealth is described in terms of land (Ruth 2:1–3, 4:1–9; Acts 4:34–

5:3), herds (Genesis 13:2; Job 1:3, 42:12), and natural products (Matthew 13:45–46). However, the writers of the Bible knew of technological intervention, and often wrote of human craftsmanship as adding to economic value (Proverbs 31:10–31; Acts 16:14–15).

Although at least one author has taken the view that the Bible is an anti-technology tract,[7] this appears to be an extreme view. The writers of the Bible seem to have believed that wise use of natural resources may include their refinement by technology. The Jewish holy buildings, the Tabernacle and Solomon's Temple, were evidently examples of state-of-the-art technology, and descriptions of the craftsmanship necessary to build them are included in the Bible (Exodus 35–39 and 1 Kings 5–6, respectively).

Life support value. Most of the economic value of natural entities mentioned in the Bible is life-support value. Even a casual reader of the Bible will be impressed by the variety of references to food and water (Genesis 1:29–30; 2 Samuel 16:1–2, 23:13–17; Matthew 12:1–4, 14:13–21; Genesis 41:53–42:2; Revelation 21:6, 22:1). The culture of the times was such that people did not take food for granted. In fact, it seems that our culture is the aberration. (One of my former students, now a high school teacher, once asked a class what the consequences would be if all green plants were eliminated. They told her not to worry—even though you couldn't garden, you could continue to buy food in grocery stores!)

Not only were the biblical writers aware of the life-support value of food, but they certainly recognized other life-support values in nature. Psalm 104, that great nature poem, speaks of life support for nonhuman organisms, rain for crops, wine and olive oil for values in addition to nutrition, and the moon as a marker for the seasons. Jonah's plant (Jonah 4:6–10) supported him by giving shelter from the heat.

Recreational value. According to Rolston, there are two kinds of recreational value in nature: as a stage for man's activity and as a production.[8] Examples of these values are hang gliding and watching a rainbow respectively. Neither kind is easily identifiable, since those who wrote the Bible seem to have had a different view of recreation than we do today. I know of no explicit examples of the former type at all, unless perhaps Peter's decision to go fishing after Christ's death (John 21:3) was motivated by a desire to obtain recreational value. Nevertheless, many people living in biblical times and places, especially those engaged in outdoor occupations, such as hunting (Genesis 10:9, 25:27), fishing (Mark 1:16–17), and shepherding (Exodus 3:1, 1 Samuel 16:11, Luke 2:8) may have obtained this sort of value from nature. Likewise, going into nature to observe it for recreational purposes does seem to have been implied in the male lover's invitation (Song of Solomon 2:10–13). It is also possible that the spiritual retreats of Moses (Exodus 3:1–2, Elijah (1 Kings 17:3–6; 19:3–18), John the Baptist (Mark 1:4–6), Jesus[9] (Matthew 4:1–11; Luke 4:42, 6:12, 9:10, 9:28, 22:29–41), and Paul (Galatians 1:17) had recreational value as well as spiritual value, and the recreational value, if it existed, may have been of either of Rolston's two sorts. However, in order to find recreational value in these passages we almost certainly need to read more into them than their authors had in mind.

A stronger case can be made that writers of the Bible were depicting nature as a production which had value. Much of Psalm 104, parts of the last portion of Job, and parts of Proverbs 30 can be taken this way. There is explicit mention of the beauty of nature in Christ's words in Matthew 6:26–29. It is true that these passages were written more for spiritual purposes than to state a view of nature, but the view seems to be there all the same. On the other hand, if there is a spiritual point to Ecclesiastes 11:7, it is less obvious, and this passage provides good evidence that the recreational value of nature was not a concept wholly foreign to the biblical writers.

Scientific value. As has already been mentioned, the Bible is a book from a prescientific age. Nonetheless, there are a number of passages which all seem to indicate clearly that to the writers or speakers nature was "interesting enough to justify being known."[10] Consider, for example, Proverbs 6:6 ("Go to the ant, thou sluggard; consider her ways, and be wise"[11]), the wisdom of Solomon in 1 Kings 4:32–33 ("And he spake of trees, from the cedar tree that is Lebanon even unto the hyssop that springeth out of the wall: he spake also of beasts, and of fowl, and creeping things, and of fishes"), Job 38:41 ("Who provideth for the raven his food? when his young ones cry unto God, they wander for lack of meat"), Proverbs 30:18–31 ("The locusts have no king, yet go they forth all of them by band"), and certain of the parables of Jesus (for example, Matthew 13:3–8 and 31–32, which discuss the sowing of seeds). Solomon, for one, certainly seems to have met Rolston's "test for an unalloyed scientist."[12] Presumably, the magi (Matthew 2:1–2) also would have, and they were amateur astronomers.

Aesthetic value. The Bible begins with the creation story, punctuated by the repeated statement, "It was good." These expressions probably are meant mostly to assert completeness and consistency with the holiness of God, but they may also imply aesthetic goodness. The end of the Bible includes a description of the new Jerusalem (Revelation 21). No doubt this description has symbolic meaning, but it is difficult to read it without also glimpsing appreciation of beauty.

The profound statements at the beginning and end of the Bible bracket more straightforward expressions of appreciation of aesthetic value in nature. The Tree of Knowledge of

Good and Evil is described as beautiful (Genesis 3:6). The Leviathan passage in Job is mostly about invulnerability, but is partly about appreciation of the beauty of the animal's construction (see Job 41:12, 18–19 and 34). Perhaps the clearest statement on aesthetic value in nature is part of the Sermon on the Mount, the comparison of the lilies of the field to Solomon (Matthew 6:28–30). Jesus said that the flowers were more glorious than the most gorgeous human clothing.

Life value. According to Rolston, "Reverence for life is commended by every great religion."[13] What, then, is the biblical basis for such reverence? To begin with, although the creation story is sketchy, it does portray the beginnings of nonhuman life explicitly (Genesis 1:11–25). The animals (apparently at least the mammals, and perhaps reptiles and amphibians), together with the birds, had an origin similar to man's (Genesis 2:7,19). Adam is described as naming them and hoping to find a companion among them (Genesis 2:20).

The story of Noah's ark includes some references to life value. The ark was designed not just for Noah and his family, but also for the animals. Both God and Noah were careful to preserve them (Genesis 6:9–8:19). One reason for preserving them must have been their life-support value for man; nevertheless, as Genesis 8:1 suggests, God was concerned not only for Noah, but also for the animals, for "every living thing." The promise not to send another flood (Genesis 8:21), moreover, was a promise not to destroy the animals, as well as not to destroy man.

Other books of the Old Testament, for example, Job, the Psalms, and the Proverbs, also display some reverence for nonhuman life. There are passages in these books that refer obliquely to life value, such as Job 39 and 41, Psalm 104, and Proverbs 30:18–31, as well as a more direct statement about a righteous person caring for his animals in Proverbs 12:10.

Finally, the New Testament contains at least two statements made by Jesus establishing value for nonhuman life. One is the pronouncement concerning God's care for birds and plants in the Sermon on the Mount (Matthew 6:25–32). The other is a reminder that the Father even knows when individual sparrows die (Matthew 10:28).

Diversity and unity values. The prophet Isaiah said, "All flesh is grass" (Isaiah 40:6)[14] and he was quoted some centuries later in 1 Peter 1:24. Although this passage may indicate a recognition of the unity of life, more probably it speaks of the mortality of man, with the implication that life's unity is peripheral. There are, nevertheless, some stronger indications of unity value in the Bible. The creation of all organisms is described in one passage (Genesis 1), and land vertebrates, and perhaps invertebrates, are described as having been created on the same day, perhaps in the same way, as man. Several of the Proverbs imply a unity to life— for instance, the comparison of eagles, snakes, and a man and a woman falling in love in Proverbs 30:19–21. Even the final fate of man and animals is considered the same by the author of Ecclesiastes (Ecclesiastes 3:18–21).

The fact that the writers of the Bible perceived some unity between man and other organisms does not mean, however, that they perceived great value in this unity. But Rolston also seems to fall short of this: "The sciences describe much natural *diversity* and also much *unity,* terms which are descriptive and yet contain dimensions of value."[15]

Such passages as the lists of clean and unclean animals (Leviticus 11; Deuteronomy 14:3–20), the discussion of animals in Job 38:39–41:34, and the lists of clever or otherwise impressive animals in Proverbs 30 seem to imply value in diversity. One explicit statement is Psalm 104:24–25: "O Lord, how manifold are thy works! in wisdom hast thou made them all: the earth is full of thy riches. So is this great and wide sea, wherein are things creeping innumerable, both small and great beasts."[16] This seems to clearly tie the diversity of God's works with his wisdom in creating them, hence recognizing the value of diversity.[17]

Although I have tried to restrict this paper to a discussion of the biblical view of nonhuman life, one passage about man deserves mention here. 1 Corinthians 12:12–31 uses the diversity of the parts of the body as a parable of the value of diversity in the church: "For as the body is one, and hath many members, and all the members of that one body, being many, are one body; so also is Christ. . . . If the whole body were an eye, where were the hearing? If the whole body were hearing, where were the smelling? But now hath God set the members every one of them in the body, as it hath pleased him" (1 Corinthians 12:12, 17–18).

Stability and spontaneity values. Rolston points out the value of regularity, repeatability, and reliability in nature, as well as the contrasting value of spontaneity and mutability. The world view of the writers of the Bible clearly included the concept of the stability of nature. Consider the regularity marked by the creation of the lights, the predictability of the "after his kind" statements of Genesis 1, and the promise of regularity after the flood (Genesis 8:21–22). The first eleven verses of Ecclesiastes and James 1:17 also make the same point. As the author of Ecclesiastes puts it: "I know that, whatsoever God doeth, it shall be for ever: nothing can be put to it, nor any thing taken from it: and God doeth it, that men should fear before him. That which hath been is now; and that which is to be hath already been; and God requireth that which is past" (Ecclesiastes 3:14–15).

Although there was recognition of permanence, there was also recognition that "the system" as a whole is impermanent. For example, the "while the earth remaineth" passage of Genesis 8:22 appears to be an escape clause. Prophecies of the end of the world occur throughout the Bible—for example, Psalm 102:26; Isaiah 34:4, 51:6; Revelation 21:1.

Weather, naturally, was recognized to be unpredictable, or spontaneous. Job 38:22–30 and the story of the sudden storm given in Mark 4:35–41 are good examples. The biblical writers also recognized that offspring are not exactly like their parents. Whatever else the story of Jacob's cattle means (Genesis 30:35–43, 31:8–13) it includes that idea. The parable of the seed (Matthew 13:3–8) used the idea of the variety of soil types. Animals are said to have to deal with unpredictability in nature in their search for food (Job 38:41). Although there are ideas of impermanence and unpredictability in the Bible, those given so far do not seem to be related to positive value.

One connection of positive value to spontaneity concerns the freedom of God's creatures. Job 39 is a celebration of wildness. The mountain goats, the wild asses, the unicorns (perhaps wild cattle), ostriches, horses, and hawks are praised for their wildness, and the point of the passage is that their freedom has been given them by God. He asks Job, "Who hath set the wild ass free?"

It may be worth mentioning that miracles, by definition, mean that an unexpected element has been introduced into nature (a wind parted the Red Sea, one meal fed a large crowd, and so forth), but a miracle, also by definition, is *supernatural*.[18] Yet this shows that God was perceived as having spontaneity value.

Dialectical value. Rolston shows a modern appreciation for dialectical value in nature. As he puts it: "Culture is carved out *against* nature but carved out *of* nature, and this is not simple to handle valuationally. Superficially, so far as nature is antagonistic and discomforting, it has disvalue. . . . With deeper insight, we do not always count environmental conductance as good and environmental resistance as bad. . . .

And environment which is entirely irenic would stagnate us. . . . All our culture, in which our classical humanity consists, and all our science, in which our modern humanity consists, has originated in the face of oppositional nature."[19] The Bible is certainly not without dialectical ideas, such as Jesus' statement about saving one's life by losing it (Matthew 16:25–26) or the sequence about tribulation working to accomplish patience, and so forth (Romans 4:3–5). In fact, the central idea of the Bible is a dialectical one—Jesus brought life forth out of death.

Does the Bible include dialectical ideas about the value of nature? At least a few. The Israelites were refined not only by Egyptian conquerors and Amalekite enemies but by wilderness privations and the struggles of taming a land. Not only are such triumphs over nature collective, but they are personal. Genesis 3:19 and Ecclesiastes 5:12 and 9:7–10 are about the rewards from combating environmental resistance.

Sacramental value. Jesus used nature as an object lesson. Examples include his parables, especially those about the kingdom. Parables in which natural objects play an important role include the parables of the sower and the seed, the tares, the mustard seed, the leaven, the pearl, and the parable of the net (all found in Matthew 13), and others. Jesus also compared himself, or his followers, to natural entities such as light (Matthew 5:14–16, John 8:12) and salt (Matthew 5:13). Thus, nature has a sacramental role in that it serves as an aid to teach us how to live.

Perhaps the most important sacramental function of nature is that it points us toward God. There are a great many statements of this sort in the Bible. The dialogue between Job and God (Job 38:1–42:6), referred to at several points above, uses God's power over nature as a demonstration of his power and wisdom. The nature poetry of Psalm

104 begins and ends by asserting that it is not a celebration of nature, but of nature's creator. Other important statements showing how nature points man toward God are Psalm 19:1–3, Romans 1:19–20, and this notable passage attributed to David: "When I consider thy heavens, the work of thy fingers, the moon and the stars, which thou hast ordained; What is man, that thou art mindful of him? and the son of man, that thou visitest him?" (Psalm 8:3–4).

Obviously no discussion of the sacramental value of nature can leave out the role of natural objects in the sacraments. The most important sacrament of the Old Testament was animal sacrifice (Genesis 4:4; Leviticus, chapters 1, 3–7; 1 Kings 8:62–64). Other natural objects were also sacrificed or put to other sacramental uses (Exodus 12:1–28, 30:22–38; Leviticus 2). (Note also the construction of the Tabernacle and the Temple, discussed above.) The central sacrifice of the New Testament was performed on a wooden cross. Shortly before it took place, Jesus had established the sacramental significance of bread and wine (Luke 22:17–20). His followers baptized with water (Acts 8:36–39).

It is also true that, in the view of the writers of the Bible, nature could be used for the wrong sacraments (Isaiah 44:9–20; Romans 1:23). However, on balance, it seems clear that the biblical view of nature was that it had great positive sacramental value. If Rolston has listed the values so that the one he perceives as most important is last, he certainly seems to be in agreement with some noted authors of the distant past.

Moral Considerability and Moral Agency

Continuing my theme of how the Bible treats the nonhuman, I wish to examine two concepts, recently delineated, which relate to the treatment of nonhuman entities by man. The first of these is moral considerability. According to Goodpaster, living things have interests; hence, morally, these interests must be taken into account in planning human activities.[20] Does this concept occur in the Bible? To some extent, yes. The above section on life value may be taken as a partial demonstration of that. The Bible does teach reverence for living things, in some cases, apparently, simply because they are alive. The dominion statements in Genesis (Genesis 1:26–28, 9:2–4), especially the former, delineate man's role as being responsible for living things, without any apparent reference to their usefulness to man.[21]

The concept of moral agency is a narrower one.[22] Watson's discussion of it outlines six criteria establishing a framework of reciprocity defining a moral agent, "a being who relates morally to others."[23] Since the Bible is rightly characterized as a homocentric book, I was surprised to note that there are some indications that people of Biblical times imputed moral agency to nonhuman animals.

The extraordinary cases of the curse on the serpent (Genesis 3:1–15) and of Balaam's she-ass (Numbers 22:22–33), supernaturally given the power of speech to admonish her master, do not seem to shed any light on the moral agency of typical animals. Two cases that may shed such light are Exodus 21:28–32 and Genesis 9:5–6, both involving a beast killing a human. The former example should probably be considered more as a means of removing the danger of a goring ox, with responsibility falling on the owner, than as an establishment of moral guilt of the ox. The latter may be a similar case, but may imply more: "And surely your blood of your lives will I require; at the hand of every beast will I require it, and at the hand of every man."

There are other possible cases of imputed moral agency, all involving punishment. One is Leviticus 20:15–16, in which the Israelites were instructed to kill any human, and any beast, involved in bestiality. In Genesis 6:6–7, God said he was sorry that he had made man and the animals, and was sending the flood as a result. A fig tree (Mark 11:12–14, 20–25) was destroyed for not producing figs, in spite of the fact that it was not the season for them. Jesus "rebuked" the wind (Mark 4:39).

Probably because of my own world view, I believe that the world view of at least some of the writers of the Bible included some concept of the moral considerability, but probably not moral agency, of nonhuman entities. I come to the latter conclusion because I find it difficult to believe that the Bible teaches anything about the moral agency of figs. The key to all the passages in the last two paragraphs, it seems to me, is symbolism. There seems to be no suggestion that animals involved in intercourse with humans are equally guilty with them, any more than the walls and buildings of Jericho were Joshua's enemy (Joshua 6) or the ark of the covenant was meant to be treated as sacred for its own sake. Non-moral agents were involved in the acts of God and man as symbols. God was not spoken of as being primarily sorry that he had made animals, but as being sorry for the acts and thoughts of men. A flood came, destroying most of both, as an act and symbol of God's total repudiation of sin. The Israelites were to destroy both animals and humans involved in bestiality for similar reasons. The story of the fig tree is, in this context, intended as an assertion of the general authority of Jesus, and seems to have been meant as an object lesson. The same seems true of the storm. Probably even the destruction of an animal that had killed a human was done to demonstrate the importance of human life, not the guilt of cows, bears, and lions.

Conclusion

The Bible is primarily about God's relationship to man. It is not, except peripherally, about other organisms. Nevertheless, reviewing the statements in the Bible about nonhuman organisms leads one to the conclusion that the writers of the Bible were aware of almost as many kinds of value as those enumerated by sophisticated contemporary thinkers like Rolston. These values in nature, moreover, were not restricted to the provision of food, shelter, and clothing, but included recreational, aesthetic, scientific, and of course, sacramental value.

With regard to the moral status of nonhuman organisms, although the biblical view seems to be that they are morally considerable, there is no clear evidence that any nonhuman organism in the Bible merited the status of a moral agent. While this position is less than some theorists call for today, it can provide a good guide for most of us.

Certainly the dominion of twentieth-century man is more extensive than that of man of Bible times. We are more widely distributed; we have more knowledge; we use nature in more ways. As inheritors, willing or not, of the Judaeo-Christian heritage, we must be moral agents who consider nature morally. It has great value.

Notes

1. Lynn White, Jr., "The Historical Roots of Our Ecological Crisis," *Science* 155 (1967): 1203–7; James Barr, "Man and Nature: The Ecological Controversy and the Old Testament," *Bulletin of the John Rylands Library* 55, no. 1 (1972): 9–32, reprinted in *Ecology and Religion in History*, ed. David Spring and Eileen Spring (New York: Harper, 1974), pp. 48–75; John Passmore, *Man's Responsibility for Nature: Ecological Problems and Western Traditions* (New York: Charles Scribner's Sons, 1974). The author thanks Central Wesleyan College and Bryan College for financial support, and Holmes Rolston III and Donald Wood for allowing him to overhear a conversation which led to the writing of this paper. He thanks these men and

an anonymous reviewer for substantial and helpful suggestions for revision, and Grammond Paul and Sandy McJunkin for making him aware of pitfalls.

2. John Black, *The Dominion of Man* (Edinburgh, U.K.: Edinburgh University Press, 1970); Conrad Bonifazi, "Biblical Roots of an Ecologic Conscience," in *This Little Planet,* ed. Michael Hamilton (New York: Scribner's, 1970), pp. 203–33; Frederick Elder, *Crisis in Eden* (Nashville, Tenn.: Abingdon Press, 1970); William G. Pollard, "God and His Creation," in *This Little Planet,* ed. Hamilton, pp. 47–76; Francis A. Schaeffer, *Pollution and the Death of Man: A Christian View of Ecology* (Wheaton, Ill.: Tyndale House, 1970); John Macquarrie, "Creation and Environment," *The Expository Times* 83, no. 1 (1971): 4–9, reprinted in *Ecology and Religion in History,* ed. Spring and Spring, pp. 32–47; René Dubos, "Franciscan Conservation Versus Benedictine Stewardship," in *A God Within* (New York: Scribner's, 1972), reprinted in *Ecology and Religion in History,* ed. Spring and Spring, pp. 114–36; Martin LaBar, "A Message to Polluters from the Bible," *Christianity Today* 28 (1974): 1186–90; Loren Wilkinson, ed., *Earthkeeping: Christian Stewardship of Natural Resources* (Grand Rapids, Mich.: Eerdmans, 1980); Wilkinson, "Cosmic Christology and the Christian's Role in Creation," *Christian Scholar's Review* 11 (1981): 18–40; Ron Elsdon, *Bent World: A Christian Response to the Environmental Crisis* (Downers Grove, Ill.: InterVarsity, 1981) are examples.

3. Gunther S. Stent, *Paradoxes of Progress* (San Francisco: Freeman, 1978). See chaps. 1 and 2 particularly.

4. Holmes Rolston III, "Values in Nature," *Environmental Ethics* 3 (1981): 113–28.

5. Biblical references are meant to be representative, not necessarily exhaustive.

6. Rolston, "Values in Nature," p. 116.

7. Jacques Ellul, *The Meaning of the City,* trans. Dennis Pardee (Grand Rapids, Mich.: Eerdmans, 1970).

8. Rolston, "Values in Nature," p. 118.

9. Sidney Lanier's poem "A Ballad of Trees and the Master" (1880), though written long after the New Testament, expresses

the idea that entering into natural surroundings was recreational for Jesus. See Sidney Lanier, *Poems* (Macon, Ga.: Middle Georgia Historical Society, 1967), p. 141. It can also be found in some hymnals, for example, *The Methodist Hymnal* (New York: Methodist Book Concern, 1935), no. 132.

10. Rolston, "Values in Nature," p. 118.

11. This and all other quotations from the Bible are from the King James Version of 1611, which, if not the best translation, has had the greatest influence. Italics in the original of such quotations have been ignored.

12. Rolston, "Values in Nature," p. 118.

13. Ibid., p. 121.

14. Similar passages are Psalms 90:5–6 and 103:15–16, and James 1:10–11.

15. Rolston, "Values in Nature," p. 123. Italics in the original.

16. The word translated as "riches" in the King James is translated as "creatures" in some more modern versions.

17. The classic anecdote on this is cited by G. Evelyn Hutchinson, "Homage to Santa Rosalia; or, Why Are There So Many Kinds of Animals?" *American Naturalist* 93 (1959): 145–59. The British biologist J. B. S. Haldane was supposedly asked by a theologian what he had learned about God from a study of nature. Haldane replied that God had "an inordinate fondness for beetles," referring to the great number of species of Coleoptera.

18. For a treatment of the relationship between nature's laws (stability) and miracles, see C. S. Lewis, *Miracles* (New York: Macmillan, 1947).

19. Rolston, "Values in Nature," pp. 126–27. Italics in the original.

20. Kenneth Goodpaster, "On Being Morally Considerable," *Journal of Philosophy* 75 (1978): 308–25. See also W. Murray Hunt, "Are *Mere Things* Morally Considerable?" *Environmental Ethics* 2 (1980): 59–65, and Goodpaster's reply, "On Stopping at Everything: A Reply to W. M. Hunt," *Environmental Ethics* 2 (1980): 281–84.

21. See note 2 for examinations of the dominion concept.

22. Richard A. Watson, "Self-Consciousness and the Rights of Nonhuman Animals and Nature," *Environmental Ethics* 1 (1979): 99–129. Anthony Povlitis, in "On Assigning Rights to

Animals and Nature," *Environmental Ethics* 2 (1980): 67–71, comments that Watson has derived his reciprocity framework from a misinterpretation of the Golden Rule (Luke 6:31–36; Matthew 7:12), which is actually meant to serve as a guide to the actions of an individual, regardless of the response. Povlitis further comments, following Julian Huxley's *The Human Crisis* (Seattle: University of Washington Press, 1963), p. 24, that the Golden Rule applies not only to our relationship to other humans but to our relationship to nature. I believe that Povlitis is correct in his view that the Golden Rule was not meant to be a guide for reciprocal conduct, but this does not prevent Watson from defining a concept based on reciprocity. As to the application of the Golden Rule to my behavior toward dogs, mosquitoes, and weeds, I am not so sure. The Golden Rule was definitely given in the context of our behavior toward humans, but I suppose that nothing in the Matthew and Luke passages rules out its application to nonhuman entities.

23. Watson, "Self-Consciousness," p. 100.

Po-keung Ip

Taoism and the Foundations of Environmental Ethics

I take it that the major task of environmental ethics is the construction of a system of normative guidelines governing man's attitudes, behavior, and action toward his natural environment. The central question to be asked is: how *ought* man, either as an individual or as a group, to behave, to act, toward nature? By *nature* I mean the nonhuman environment man finds himself in. Surely, a question of this sort presupposes the appropriateness of the application of moral, ethical concepts to nature, namely, stones, fish, bears, trees, water, and so on. Questions about the legitimacy and meaningfulness of such an application automatically arise. However, here I presume such legitimacy without arguing for it.[1]

Any viable environmental ethics, it seems to me, should provide adequate answers to three questions: (1) What is the nature of nature? (2) What is man's relationship to nature? (3) How should man relate himself to nature? Taoism gives reasonably good answers to these questions and is, in this sense, capable of providing a metaphysical foundation for environmental ethics.

Science and Ethics

Contemporary environmental crises, such as pollution of various sorts, overusage of natural resources, and extinction of rare species, force us to reconsider exactly what the relationships between man and nature are. At the same time they compel us to reflect once again on what sort of attitudes we ought to have toward nature. The kinds of questions raised here are both scientific and ethical. On the one hand, they are scientific because only recently has man come to realize how ignorant he is of the natural surrounding he is in. It is certainly an irony to twentieth-century man that even though modern science has made tremendous strides in probing both the very large and the very small, it has little to say about the middle, that is, our surrounding ecosphere. The still immature state of the environmental sciences sadly bears this out. On the other hand, the questions envisaged here are clearly ethical in both the descriptive and the normative senses. First, we need to understand how man actually conceives his relationship with nature. This is clearly an empirical problem that invites both sociological as well as historical studies. However, we also need to go beyond these empirical questions and ask ourselves whether such attitudes are morally justified. This inevitably involves us in the problems of moral criteria.

I regard both the scientific and ethical approaches to our environmental problems to be vitally important. Both should work closely with the other. Both need the help of the other. Without either, our understanding of environmental problems must remain very limited and incomplete. But what sort of relationship should science and ethics have? I do not try to enter into this thorny problem here.[2] It is important to note, however, that by urging a close working relationship between science and ethics, I am not attempting to *derive* ethics from science. I take the position, without arguing for it, that ethics can never be derived from science, if *derived* is understood in the logical sense of deduction. That this is so is due to the fact that one can never derive *ought* from *is*—a too-familiar problem in moral philosophy. The sense in which I say that ethics should work closely with science is this: suppose we have a system of ethics, *E*, which is capable of generating a set of normative guidelines, *G*. Suppose that *G* in conjoining with the knowledge of the situation in which the agent is about to take action yields morally acceptable attitudes and actions. This set of attitudes and actions is not only morally acceptable, but is also, according to the knowledge available at the time, workable or realizable. In other words, the relationship between science and ethics is an oblique one. Scientific knowledge only supports ethics indirectly in the way that it provides evidence that the set of actions and attitudes "derivable" from the ethical system in question is workable, realizable.

Let me give a brief example. Suppose we have an ethics which exhorts people to act selflessly regardless of causes and occasions. Scientific results may suggest, however, that self-interest is a primary motivation of human behavior and action. In this case, we have an ethics which runs counter to the body of evidence concerning human nature arrived at by scientific research. We say that such ethics is not supported by science and hence is not involved in the kind of working relationship that we hope for between the two. On the other hand, if we have an ethics which is not only compatible with science, but also receives support from it (in the sense explained), then we say that we have reason to believe that it is plausible.

Two concepts will be useful in my discussion. I take an ethics to be *minimally coherent* if and only if (1) it is coherent and (2) it is compatible with science. An ethics is *maximally coherent* if and only if (1) it is minimally coherent and (2) it receives support from science. The minimally coherent ethics is a weak version of environmental ethics. The maximally coherent ethics, which requires more scientific data, and hence more research, presumably is harder to construct. Due to inadequate ecological information concerning the man-nature relationship, nevertheless, I think the kind of ethics that is workable at present is the minimally coherent one. If such understanding is correct, the first step toward an adequate theory for environmental ethics depends on the possibility of establishing such a minimally coherent ethics. In the light of such understanding, I show that Taoism, as chiefly represented by the teachings of Lao Tzu and Chuang Tzu, can provide us with such an ethic.

The Taoist Conception of Nature

Recall the three questions posed at the beginning of the paper, namely, what is the nature of nature? What is the nature of the man-nature relationship? What are the right attitudes toward nature? The first two questions are clearly metaphysical in nature and the last one is ethical. Let us see how Taoism responds to these questions.

To understand the Taoist conception of nature, one must start with the notion of *Tao*. Using a mystical and poetical language, Lao Tzu in *Tao Té Ching* gives a rich but at times amorphous representation of how nature works. This is done by means of the notion of *Tao*. At the very beginning of *Tao Té Ching*, it is said:

> The Tao (Way) that can be told is not the eternal Tao,
> The name that can be named is not the eternal name,
> The nameless is the origin of Heaven and Earth. (Chap. 1)[3]

In other places, we are also told that "Tao is eternal and has no name" (chap. 32) and that

There was something undifferentiated and yet complete,
which existed before Heaven and Earth.
Soundless and formless, it depends on nothing and does not
  change,
It operates everywhere and is free from danger,
It may be considered the mother of the Universe,
I do not know its name; I call it Tao. (Chap. 25)

From similar utterances in *Tao Té Ching*, we gather that *Tao* has the following attributes: it is nameless, intangible, empty, simple, all-pervasive, eternal, life-sustaining, nourishing.[4] Indeed, for Lao Tzu, *Tao* stands for the ultimate reality of nature. Unlike *Tien* (Heaven) and *Ti* (God),[5] *Tao* is not anything like a creator god. Rather it is a totally depersonalized concept of nature.

The namelessness of *Tao* is due to its infinite nature, since Lao Tzu believes that only finite things can be attached to a name. To give a name to a thing is to individuate it and to give it a definite identity. However, *Tao* by virtue of its infinite nature certainly rejects all names. In other words, *Tao* cannot be exhaustively individuated in the domain of empirical beings, though the latter owe their existence to *Tao*. Hence, *Tao* is not characterizable in any finite manner. Therefore, although we can, in a sense, say we "know" *Tao* by knowing this or that finite being, yet the knowledge thus arrived at is very incomplete. In this way, the nature of *Tao* is at best indeterminable insofar as human knowledge is concerned.

There is also a dynamic side of *Tao*. We are told that "reversion is the action of *Tao*" (chap. 40). *Tao* is also depicted as a process of change and transformation. In fact, everything in the universe is the result of self- and mutual transformations which are governed by the dialectical interactions of *Tao*'s two cosmic principles—*Ying* and *Yang*[6]—which explain the rhythmic processes which constitute the natural world.

Since *Tao* nourishes, sustains, and transforms beings, a natural relationship is built between them. This relationship is best understood if we understand the meaning of the *Té* of *Tao*. *Té* signifies the potency, the power, of *Tao* that nourishes, sustains, and transforms beings. As a result, the nourishment, development, and fulfillment of beings are the consequence of *Té*. Because of the nature of *Té*, it is both a potency as well as a virtue, and by virtue of the possession of *Té*, *Tao* is itself virtuous as well. Since *Té* is internalized in all beings in the universe, there is no problem of relating beings in the world. Indeed, things are related to each other not only metaphysically but also morally. The *Té* of *Tao* provides the essential connections. Man, being a member of beings, is without exception internally linked to *Tao* as well as to everything else. Moreover, being endowed with *Té*, man is also endowed with the capacity of doing virtuous things toward his cosmic counterparts. Thus, a crucial metaphysical linkage between man and nature is established. In the Taoist world view, there is no unbridgeable chasm between man and nature, because everything is inherently connected to everything else. The *Tao* is not separated from the natural world of which it is the source. In Taoism, therefore, chaos is impossible.

The moral imperative to be virtuous toward nature is made possible by another feature of *Tao*, impartiality. According to Lao Tzu, *Tao* "being all embracing, is impartial" (chap. 16). *Tao* is impartial in the sense that everything is to be treated on an equal footing. To use a more apt term, everything which is is seen as being "ontologically equal."[7] Man receives no special attention or status from *Tao*. Homocentrism is simply an alien thing in the Taoist axiological ordering of beings. As a matter of fact, the Taoist holds that there is a kind of egalitarian axiology of beings. The notion of ontological and axiological equality of beings receives further elaborations in the hands of Chuang Tzu. For Chuang

Tzu, beings are ontologically equal because they are formed as a result of a process of self- and mutual transformations. The alleged individuality and uniqueness of beings can be determinable only in such process. Everything is related to everything else through these processes of self- and mutual transformations.[8]

The Doctrine of Wu Wei

Acknowledging the fact that man-nature is an inherently connected whole, and that man and other beings, animated or otherwise, are ontologically as well as axiologically equal, the question of how man should behave or act toward his natural surroundings is readily answerable, for the Taoist would take the doctrine of *wu wei* as the proper answer to this question.

Although the doctrine of *wu wei* is relatively well-known, care must be taken as to how one construes the meaning of *wu wei*. I am taking a position which is at variance with the classical rendition. A majority of writers, to my knowledge, translate the meaning of *wu wei* as "inaction,"[9] but I think there is a better way of translating it which is more coherent with the system of thought presented in *Tao Té Ching* and other representative Taoist texts. Perhaps the translation of *wu wei* as nonaction is the result of relying too heavily on the literal understanding of the meanings of the words *wu* and *wei*. Literally, *wu* means "not"; *wei*, on the other hand, means "action" or "endeavor." However, the meaning of *wu wei* need not literally be translated as "inaction." The reasons are as follows. Although we are told that "Tao invariably takes no action [*wu wei*],[10] and yet there is nothing left undone" (chap. 37), given that *Tao* nourishes, sustains, and fulfills, *Tao* is invariably action-in-itself. To say *Tao wu wei* here is tantamount to saying that *Tao* acts in accordance with its own nature. Since *Tao* is action-in-itself, it certainly requires no additional action to act. To say *Tao* takes no action can best be understood as *Tao* taking no *exogenous* action to act, since such action would be redundant.

This construal of *wu wei* indeed has other textual support as well. For example, in characterizing the sage, Lao Tzu says that he

Deal[s] with things before they appear.
Put[s] things in order before disorder arises. . . .
A tower of nine storeys begins with a heap of earth.
The journey of a thousand *li* starts from where one stands,
He who takes an action fails.
He who grasps things loses them.
For this reason the sage takes no action and therefore does not
    fail.

(Chap. 64)

To make sense of the above paragraph, *wu wei* should not be interpreted as nonaction. To so interpret would make it very difficult to make sense of the phrases, "Deal[s] with things before they appear. Put[s] things in order before disorder arises." Surely, not only are they not nonaction, they are indeed well-planned and deliberative actions. Moreover, when Lao Tzu says, "A tower of nine storeys begins with a heap of earth. The journey of a thousand *li* starts from where one stands," he seems to be saying that things simply work in accordance with the laws of nature. Anyone who tries to do things in violation of the laws of nature is doomed to failure. Therefore, the statements, "He who takes an action fails" and "the sage takes no action and therefore does not fail," are consistently interpreted as "he who takes action in violation of the laws of nature fails" and "the sage acts in accordance with the laws of nature and therefore does not fail." The sage, being the ideal Taoist man, surely understands the *Tao* well and is thus capable of not acting against nature.[11]

The moral to be drawn from the doctrine of *wu wei* is clear and straightforward, given our interpretation of the meaning of *wu wei*. That is, insofar as ecological action is concerned, the Taoist's recommendation is so simple that it almost amounts to a truism: act in accordance with nature. However, one should be reminded of the fact that such a proposal is well supported both by the metaphysical and axiological conceptions of the man-nature relation. It is exactly this kind of metaphysical grounding that an environmental ethic needs.

Conclusion: *The Taoist Reversion*

Western man inherited from the Enlightenment legacy a conception of nature which is patently anti-environmentalistic. The world is depicted, chiefly through the work of Descartes, as a big machine consisting only of extended matter. It has no life of its own and no value of its own. Its value can only be defined in terms of human needs and purposes. It does not have intrinsic value of any sort, but has only instrumental value defined in terms of human desires. Man, being the possessor of mind, can willfully subject this allegedly lifeless world to his desires and purposes. The extreme consequence of such homocentrism is the ruthless and unlimited exploitation of the environment.

Such an attitude assumes a clear dichotomy between subjectivity and objectivity. On the subjective side, we find man with his feelings, desires, sentiments, passions, reasons, purposes, and sensations, all of these regarded as needing to be satisfied, fulfilled, or worthy of preserving and cultivating. On the objective side, we find the nonhuman world totally devoid of any sentience, functioning blindly according to mechanical laws. Such a machinelike world certainly cannot have any value and worth of its own except as a means to the satisfaction and fulfillment of human needs and wants. Such human needs and wants could range from the most noble to the most mean, from the purely aesthetic to the cognitively epistemic and to the practically technological. The physical world is there for us to comprehend (Greek philosophers), to experiment with (Francis Bacon), to transform (Karl Marx), and to exploit for material goods (Adam Smith and Milton Friedman).

Nevertheless, the man-nature relationships envisaged here are at best external and instrumental ones. The world is simply something out there, ready to be subjected to human control and use. It is simply an "otherness." As the Enlightenment teaches us, there is no internal link between it and ourselves. We do not feel that it is part of us, nor do we feel that we are part of it. We are cast into a seemingly unsurpassable gap between subject and object, between man and nature.

To transcend this human predicament, we need a philosophy which can break this metaphysical barrier that separates man from his world, one which can reconnect the essential link which has been mistakenly severed for so long between human and nonhuman counterparts. We need a philosophy which can attribute values to nonhuman objects independently of human needs. That is, nonhuman beings should be regarded as having intrinsic values of their own rather than having only extrinsic or instrumental values. Moreover, we also need a philosophy which can tell us that we are part of a universe whose parts mutually nourish, support, and fulfill each other.

It seems to me that one philosophy which satisfies the above mentioned features is the Taoist philosophy we have been discussing. Most important of all, one cannot find in it the metaphysical schism that divides subject and object, for the supposed gap between man and nature simply has no place in the Taoist conception of the man-nature relationship. Subject and object, through self- and mutual transformations, are metaphysically fused and unified. Moreover, the thesis of ontological equality of beings, and hence the axiological equality of beings, completely annihilates the kind of homocentrism which is representative of the Enlightenment world view. In addition, it also opens up the possibility of ascribing values to nonhuman objects regardless of the latter's usefulness to human beings. Thus, a theory of intrinsic value for nature is indeed forthcoming within the Taoist framework. These features are vitally important to the construction of environmental ethics of any sort, and are, I believe, capable of providing the necessary metaphysical underpinnings upon which an environmental ethics has to rest.

Taoism, moreover, is compatible with science and is thus capable of providing a minimally coherent ethics. First, it is not anti-scientific, for despite all its mystical overtones, Taoism is in fact a version of naturalism. The doctrine of *wu wei* implicitly entails a notion of observation which is germane to science.[12] Second, ecology as a science teaches us the interdependence of all life forms and nonliving things. It takes man as only one part of the interdependent whole. Every member of this intricately integrated complex is, in a very real sense, ecologically equal because each member depends on all others for survival, sustenance, and fulfillment. Analogously, the Taoist concept of ontological equality undoubtedly expresses the same idea, although in a more metaphysical way.

Note also that in Taoist metaphysics, the notion of axiological equality comes together with the notion of ontological equality. This is due to the fact that in Taoist metaphysics fact and value are fused together, just as subject and object are. Such metaphysical unification of value and fact is crucial in giving us a foundation upon which we can bring science and ethics together. It also makes it possible and meaningful to say that science and ethics coheres in this metaphysical sense. Although it seems presumptuous to assert that the Taoist ideas anticipate cognate concepts in modern ecology, nevertheless, one certainly cannot deny that the insights of the Taoist are explicitly acknowledged and endorsed by the latter.

Notes

1. Tom Regan recently has given a detailed discussion on this issue in "The Nature and Possibility of an Environmental Ethic," *Environmental Ethics* 3 (1981): 19–34.
2. See Don Marietta, Jr.'s "The Interrelationships Between Ecological Science and Environmental Ethics," *Environmental Ethics* 1 (1979): 195–207.
3. All quotations from *Tao Te Ching* are from Chan Wing-Tsit, *A Source Book in Chinese Philosophy* (Princeton, N.J.: Princeton University Press, 1963), pp. 139–73. They are identified in the text by chapter number.
4. See *Tao Te Ching*, chaps. 1, 74, 21, 35, 4, 6, 32.
5. The origins of the notions of *Ti* (God) and *Tien* (Heaven) were closely tied with ancestor worship in ancient China. *Ti* apparently represented a personal god and was supposed to be the perennial source of life. However, it was subsequently replaced by a less personalistic notion of *Tien*. The latter was a highly naturalistic notion which had no strong religious connotation, but was mainly used to stand for the physical sky. See Chang Chung-ying, "Chinese Philosophy: A Characterization," in *Introduction to Chinese Philosophy*, ed. A. Naess and A. Hannay (Oslo: Universitetsforlaget, 1972), pp. 141–65.
6. See Derk Bodde, "Harmony and Conflict in Chinese Philosophy," in A. F. Wright, ed., *Studies in Chinese Thought* (Chicago: University of Chicago Press, 1953), p. 121.
7. For more on the notion of ontological equality, see Chang, "Chinese Philosophy," p. 149.

8. For more on the self- and mutual-transformation of beings, see *Chuang Tzu*, chapter 2, in Chan, *Source Book*.
9. See Fung Yu-lan, *A History of Chinese Philosophy*, vol. 1, trans. D. Bodde (Princeton: Princeton University Press, 1952), p. 187; Chan, *Source Book*.
10. I systematically replaced *wu wei* in all places in Chan's original translations.
11. For other textual evidence to support my interpretation, see *Haai Nan Tzu*, quoted in J. Needham, *Science and Civilization in China*, vol. 2 (Cambridge: Cambridge University Press, 1956), p. 51 and *Chuang Tzu* in Chan, *Source Book*.
12. Needham incidentally holds such a view; see Colin A. Ronan, *The Shorter Science and Civilization in China*, vol. 1 (Cambridge: Cambridge University Press, 1978), p. 98.

Iqtidar H. Zaidi

On the Ethics of Man's Interaction with the Environment: An Islamic Approach

W hereas in the quest of maximizing benefits from his environment man has had an excellent record, he has in the process also created serious environmental disruptions. The problems range from "the spectacular, such as atmospheric pollution and water contamination, to the insidious, such as slow rise in the D.D.T. levels in some living species associated with human food chain."[1] Kates reports that presently in the United States technological hazards account for fifteen to twenty percent of human mortality with an associated economic cost and losses of $50–75 billion annually. In the case of less developed countries, due to the lack of systematic studies of technological hazards, Kates finds it difficult to estimate such losses precisely, but giving due allowance to the lack of health care and other services, he observes that the losses can be expected to approach or even exceed U.S. levels in heavily urbanized areas.[2]

The increasing magnitude and proliferation of the undesirable byproducts of man's interaction with the environment can indeed be ascribed to human failings as well as foulings—namely, greedy manipulation of the environment, mismanagement of resources, extravagance, and ignorance of the complexity of the ecosystem—not to mention the intended impact of man's chosen actions, which may also be detrimental. Good examples of what happens when developmental processes are generated without any ethical infeed are not difficult to find.[3]

Our ecological crisis is in fact a moral crisis and needs a moral solution. Put more directly, what we need is a set of principles that are environmentally relevant and socially responsible. What should be the source of the ethical principles we are looking for? This indeed is a moot question and will be discussed in the following section. One thing, however, is amply clear. We need principles which emphasize ethical ideals and at the same time encourage improvement in material well-being. Such a set of principles cannot be properly formulated by any individual or a group of individuals, however modern in terms of abilities and skill they may be, unless it is linked with a metaphysical dimension. Man-made laws cannot be entirely aboveboard in subordinating selfish desires for economic, social, and political progress. Hence, in order to deal effectively with our ecological crises, we have to find ethical principles embedded in a religious matrix, a framework properly linked with divine doctrines. Furthermore, it must be noted that we are seeking a religious matrix that maintains man's position as an ecologically dominant being, a world view well founded in geographic literature.[4]

In this paper I argue that Islam provides us with a useful religious matrix for developing proper ethical principles because it provides a formula for the improvement of human well-being within the theomorphic framework. Islam as preached by Muhammad (S.A.), the last prophet, is the chosen religion of God, and is the perfected version of the same faith and tradition as was preached by all other apostles predating him, namely, Adam, Noah, Abraham, Moses, and Jesus (A.S.).[5] Islam's fundamental dogma is *At-Tawhid*, the formula of unity and totality. Obviously then, a doctrine rooted in Islamic philosophy must affirm the doctrine of Divine Unity, which is reflected in some way in all the traditions before Islam.[6]

Operationally, man-environment interaction implies a behavioral-functional relationship between man and his environment, which is built upon a complex process of decision-action generated by his world view. Thus, the most important questions that we are concerned with are: (1) how the world view is defined within the matrix of the Islamic philosophy of life, and (2) how the decision-action processes operate within that matrix. Each of these questions is examined in appropriate sections. Parenthetically, it may be mentioned here that the term *environment* is used here in the broadest sense to include physical, biological, man-made, social, and economic reality. Nevertheless, in this paper more frequent references are directed to the resource processes which are apparently most responsible for the disruption of environmental quality.

The main source from which arguments have been drawn is the Holy Quraan. The Revelation of Islam was given in the form of this sacred book, and its importance with reference to the questions discussed in this paper cannot be exaggerated. Prophets' and imams' traditions have also been used to substantiate the arguments.

The Hypothesis of Ethical Infeed

The search for ethical principles for the management of the processes in man-environment interactions is not new. Efforts have constantly been made in this direction, particularly since the environmental crusade was launched in the

United States toward the end of the 1960s. The United Nations Conference on Human Environment (held in Stockholm in June 1972) provided further impetus for research and formulations along these lines.[7] Simmons has skillfully summarized various views relating to the ethical principles. Heavily drawing on the works of Black, Boulding, Toynbee, and Bruhn, Simmons concludes that there is a need to reevaluate the idea of continued progress, a *work ethic* strongly implanted by Protestant capitalism in the nineteenth century and followed in both capitalistic as well as socialist countries.[8] He observes that it is the time for ethics and science to unite to produce a guide to individual and collective behavior which lays stress on the quality of life rather than the mere production of goods in the developed countries.[9]

White in his study of the historical roots of the ecological crisis finds that the current world view which governs the man-environment relationship is associated with the Judeo-Christian tradition, which encourages man to exploit nature without any restriction. He goes on to argue that both present science and present technology are so "tinctured with orthodox Christian arrogance toward nature that no solution for our ecologic crisis can be expected from them alone," unless we find a new religion or rethink our old one (that is, Christianity) and "we reject the Christian axiom that nature has no reason for existence save to serve man."[10] Toynbee is so disgusted with the wanton exploitation of the earth's resources that he goes a step further. He rejects the usefulness of the monotheistic religions altogether, and, instead, pleads for reversion to pantheism.[11]

Both White and Toynbee seem to be building their respective theses on the assumption that had the concept of a designed earth for the use of man not been present in the Judaic and Christian scriptures, man would have behaved better; he would have made peace with nature and would have not exploited the earth's resources ruthlessly. This assumes a kind of human nature which does not err and which is free from selfish desires (such as greed and lust) for the economic and political power needed to support and expand man's physical, psychic, and territorial area of influence and action. Both men seem to be ignoring the historical fact that the people, in the quest of material progress, have disregarded the ethics of their own philosophy of life. This has happened even in those societies which have traditionally regarded nature as sacred. For example, Tuan points out that in ancient China the philosophy of man's harmony with nature was demonstrably violated in the quest for material progress; and since 1949 this philosophy itself has been completely abandoned.[12] Interestingly enough White himself presents an alternative Christian view based on Saint Francis's interpretation of the man-nature relationship in Christianity.[13] This shows that there is nothing intrinsically wrong with the Judeo-Christian axiom of a "designed Earth." The error lies in its interpretation. Nevertheless, the alternative view as argued by White is at the other extreme. It pleads for the spiritual autonomy of all parts of nature. Such a love of nature emanates from the romantic passion for wild nature, and may itself be a selfish attitude.[14]

Black presents a more balanced view. He traces the idea of man's stewardship of the earth in the Judaic and Christian scriptures.[15] But under the thrust of a secularized intellectual and technological atmosphere in the West, where the hypothesis of God had become unnecessary to many scientists and thinkers as early as the late eighteenth century, this idea of stewardship has not been properly interpreted. An important derivative of this theme is the philosophy of symbiotic relationship between man and his environment. For example, to Simmons "it appears healthier for man to regard the planet less as a set of commodities for use and more as a community of which he forms a part."[16] Such an ecosystem model of the man-environment relationship, as Bennet suggests, is "inappropriate" and "awkward" because it does not properly take care of the social-behavioral and valuational factors involved in the human use of natural resources.[17]

Indeed, the solution of the ecological crisis, as White also advocates, lies in a religious approach, not because its origin lies in religion, but because it is believed that a religious approach (like that of Islam) offers the best solution.[18] Such an approach would maintain man's position on the earth as ecologically dominant, but at the same time regulate his behavior by clearly defined measures of reward and punishment, both in this as well as in the other world. Put in other words, what is needed is a religious matrix in which the concept of man's stewardship implies management of the resource processes, as a temporary guardian, so as conscientiously and creatively to enrich, rather than degrade, the quality of the environment for human living. So long as we continue to work with man-made laws in utter disregard of the divine principles, a judicious and unbiased management of the earth's resources cannot be expected: "Peace in human society and preservation of human values are impossible without peace with natural and spiritual orders and respect for the immutable supra-human realities which are the source of all that is called human values."[19]

Whereas Muslims are required to emphasize ethical and spiritual qualities, in the West a different kind of ethical quality exists, one in harmony with Western civilization. Occidental spiritual excellence lies primarily in the successes brought about in the field of economic development. In both capitalistic and socialistic systems, as mentioned earlier, the emphasis is on material progress at any cost.[20]

The Islamic World View

Yi Fu Tuan defines *world view* as "conceptualized experience, . . . an attitude or belief system." *Attitude,* as he explains, is "primarily a cultural stance, a position one takes
vis-a-vis the world." He asserts that "world view . . . is necessarily constructed out of a people's social and physical
setting."[21]

Within a secular framework, this is perhaps the best way to
define the world view of a people in a specific space and time
context. At the universal order of the scale, however, the most
useful part of Tuan's definition lies in the idea that world
view is an attitude toward or a belief system related to the
environment, or a position that one takes vis-à-vis the world.
According to this, what I call a "belief system model," the
world view of a people, can be best defined in terms of a
religious matrix in which Tuan's "conceptualized experience" serves as a feedback loop. The position that one takes
vis-à-vis the world in Islam is not defined in terms of conceptualized experience, but rather as a belief system based entirely on revelation, a properly structured framework of
thought and action as ordained by God through the Quraan.

According to the Islamic world view, God created the
earth and heavens for the use of man.[22] But man has to work
in accordance with the code of ethics provided within the
system, or else in the case of deviations, man earns God's
wrath, and the authorities in the Islamic state are delegated
with the power to take appropriate action against such de-
viants in accordance with the legal provisions derived from
the Quraan and the Prophet's tradition. The following verse
provides a good example of the way man is warned by God:
"Then We appoint you Viceroys in the Earth after them, that
We might see how you behave."[23]

"Creation of man" is termed in the Quraan as the appointment of the viceroy of God on earth.[24] With his intellectual faculty and power of discovery and invention, man is supposed to subdue the earth and utilize all natural resources so that he is able to achieve the ultimate aim for which the process of creation began: "to develop his own Conscious Self as the focus of all that was in the Universe, hidden or apparent man was ordained to be the most compact and comprehensive representative of God's attributes and excellences," which is submission (*Ubudiat* or Islam). Although angels (intellectual-physical processes functioning in the process of creation) and other material and nonmaterial celestial and terrestrial beings also "represent the Divine attributes in some way or the other, yet none of them is as compact and comprehensive in its representative status as man, and hence they are termed in Quraan differently as 'signs of God.' "[25]

It is, therefore, important to note that one of the distinguishing features of Islam lies in the role that it assigns to intellect and its reflection on the human level, that is, reason. Islam emphasizes that reason must play its role even in the domain of faith; it tries to remove the obstacles that passion can place in the way of objective reasoning so that the believer is able to penetrate into the very heart of the faith which is the Unity of the Divine Essence. When human reason is healthy and balanced, it must lead to *Tawhid* rather than denial of the Divine.[26] There are a number of verses in the Quraan which make it abundantly clear that God has created the earth for the service of man, but at the same time, man is also constantly reminded that the earth with whatsoever is on its surface, in its interior, and in its atmosphere belongs to Almighty Allah, so that He gives all the individual human beings (as His Vice-regents), without any distinction or discrimination, the right of ownership of the natural resources for the purpose of their utilization and development. For example: "Unto Allah [belongeth] whatsoever is in the heavens and whatsoever is in the earth; and whether ye make known what is in your minds or hide it, Allah will bring you to account for it. He will forgive whom He will and He will punish whom He will. Allah is able to do all things."[27]

Perhaps the most important attribute of the Earth which we have to remember while interacting with it is that, in order to enable the execution of the divine plan, God creates everything on the earth well measured in accordance with the respective needs of time, space, and individuals. To quote from the Quraan:

> And the earth have We spread out, and placed therein firm hills, and caused each seemly thing to grow therein [well measured].
> And We have given unto you livelihoods therein, and unto those for whom ye provide not.[28]

Furthermore, in the clearest possible terms God forbids us from acts which might lead to environmental disruption. For example:

> That ye exceed not the measure;
> But observe the measure strictly, nor fall short thereof.
> And the earth hath He appointed for [His] creatures.[29]

The phenomena of nature are constantly referred to in the Quraan as signs of God to be contemplated by the believers.[30] The term *sign* implies a stimulus to movement or action.[31]

If a pattern of thought such as that described above governs the human behavior vis-à-vis the earth, it becomes the duty of the leadership in an Islamic state to control human actions so that environmental quality is not allowed to deteriorate. In Islam, a person's ownership of the land is allowed only as long as he is working well in producing goods and services for the general public. If, in some way, he fails to do so or disregards his responsibilities toward the community and its environment, his right to own that piece of land ceases. This is in addition to the fact that he is also accountable before God.[32]

An excellent description of the Islamic world view is presented by Ali (A.S.), the Prophet's closest associate and the greatest Islamic scholar and thinker of his age, and I think it is useful to quote it in full:

> Verily, this world is a house of truth for those who look into it deeply and carefully, an abode of peace and rest for those who understand its ways and moods, and it is the best working ground for those who want to procure rewards for life hereafter. It is a place of acquiring knowledge and wisdom for those who want to acquire them, a place of worship for friends of God and Angels. It is a place where prophets receive revelation of the Lord. It is a place for virtuous people and saints to do good deeds and to be assigned with rewards for the same; only in this world they could trade with God's Favours and Blessings, and only while living here they could barter their good deeds with His Blessings and Rewards. Where else could this all be done?[33]

Parenthetically, it should be mentioned that Ali (A.S.) gave this description of the world when he heard someone who was abusing and blaming the world.

Thus, it becomes abundantly clear that according to the Islamic world view man is ecologically dominant, but unlike materialist schools of thought he is not permitted to misuse the bounties of God on earth and engage in excesses. He has to do good deeds in order to acquire a better position in the life hereafter. This world is only a temporary abode for man. As Ali (A.S.) observes, "God has created galaxies and the earth not without any design, purpose or program. A Universe without plan, purpose or program is the idea of infidels and the heathens who are condemned to the fire of Hell."[34]

The Decision-Action Processes in Islam

As discussed earlier, according to Islamic world view man dominates over nature only by virtue of his theomorphic makeup. He, as the viceroy of God on earth, is the instrument of his will and that "grace and justice" are *a priori* factors manifested in his "will and intention."[35] Grace and justice are the two interrelated aspects (one manifested by the other) of one of his relative attributes, namely "his universal love."[36] Muhammad (S.A.) as the most perfect being is characterized in the Quraan as the representative of this principal attribute of God; he is the Lord Cherisher and Muhammad (S.A.) is his grace.[37] God describes him as a person of great *khulq* (the closest term in English is *character*).[38]

It is this *khulq* of the Prophet (S.A.) that sets the standard for the ethical excellence, which we must strive to achieve as best as possible, and it is this *khulq* that must govern the decision-action processes in all spheres of life including our interaction with the environment. It is important to remember that the basis of this *khulq* is justice; and justice cannot be practiced without *taqwa* (the closest equivalent in English is *piety*) and knowledge. Put in other words, justice, *taqwa* and knowledge are the core concepts on which Islamic adminstrative policies must be formulated, the policies which manifest obedience to God. As Ali (A.S.) puts it: "Islam means obedience to God; Obedience to God means having sincere faith in Him; such a faith means to believe in His power; a belief in His power means recognizing and accepting His Majesty; acceptance of His Majesty means fulfilling the obligations laid down by Him; and fulfillment of obligation means action.[39]

Thus, faith in Islam means action, action which must be administered within the framework of the *khulq* of the Prophet (S.A.), whose obedience is in fact obedience to God, who orders obedience to Divine Leadership as well.[40] Within such a matrix of decision-action processes, the main causes leading to the undesirable effects of man's interaction with the environment like greed, extravagance, ignorance, careless use of technology, and the mismanagement of resources can be properly controlled.

The Ethical Principles: Justice, Taqwa, *and Knowledge*

In Islam justice is emphasized as a fundamental principle of faith, second only to the belief in his unity. As explained earlier, it means providing in accordance with the capacity or merit of the recipient. Injustices have been condemned in strongest terms; for example: "We verily sent Our messengers with clear proofs, and revealed with them the Scripture and the Balance, that mankind may observe right measure; and He revealed iron, wherein is mighty power and [many] uses for mankind, and that Allah may know him who helpeth Him and [His messengers] though unseen. Lo! Allah is Strong, Almighty."[41]

In his famous letter, a masterpiece on administration, Ali (A.S.), in his position as the caliph of the Islamic state, reminds Malik-i-Ashtar (his governor in Egypt) of his responsibility for adopting a policy based on equity and justice. He should be above "self," Ali writes, and regard every tyrant and oppressor as the enemy of God. Since these enemies are usually from among the most powerful and important personages, he has a special responsibility to protect the rights of the poor people and safeguard their welfare. Malik-i-Ashtar is told that as governor of Egypt he cannot claim any immunity from even the minor errors of commission or omission on the excuse that he is engrossed with major problems of the state, even when he may have carried them out well.[42]

Justice and injustice, according to the Quraan, are the main yardsticks by which human virtues and vices are judged by God and by man.[43] In Islam, no individual or group, at any level, local, provincial, national, or international, is permitted to exploit resources in such a way as to cause harm to an other's well-being, including environmental quality.

Taqwa (piety) relates to the entire range of conduct rooted in absolute surrender to the Will of God. Every Muslim is required to observe *taqwa* in all kinds of decision and action. The following verse from the Quraan presents good examples of the way Allah commands the people to observe *taqwa*: "O Children of Adam! We have revealed unto you raiment to conceal your shame, and splendid vesture, but the raiment of restraint from evil [*taqwa*], that is best. This is of the revelations of Allah; that they may remember."[44]

In Islam, knowledge is the source of faith and human superiority over other creatures of the universe. From the Islamic standpoint, man started his life with knowledge and light. After his creation, the first thing with which the Creator blessed Adam (A.S.) was knowledge of things, which is a mark of distinction for mankind. Knowledge is a speciality of leadership; and man, being at the top of the hierarchy of creatures, must secure it.[45] "And He taught Adam all the names, then showed them to the angels, saying: Inform me of the names of these if ye are truthful. They said: Be glorified. We have no knowledge saving that which thou has taught us. Lo, Thou, only Thou, art the Knower, the Wise."[46]

The very first revelation of the Prophet sheds light on the place and importance of knowledge in the Islamic society:

Read: In the name of thy Lord who createth
Createth man from a clot.
Read: And thy Lord is the Most Bounteous,
Who teacheth by the pen.
Teacheth man that which he knew not.[47]

Thus, Islam has laid great emphasis on securing knowledge. According to the Prophet (S.A.), seeking knowledge is required of all Muslim men and women, even if they have to go to far-off places and have to put up with the difficulties of life in a strange land. God creates a clear distinction between those who possess knowledge and those who are ignorant; other things being equal, these two categories of people are not considered as equal in status.[48] However, it is important to note that human knowledge is not regarded as perfect,[49] and it is because of this imperfection of man's knowledge that it is so important in Islamic society for man to be advised to pray, "My Lord! increase me in knowledge."[50]

Such a conspicuous stress on securing knowledge in Islam does not mean a kind of intellectual attainment which is useful only for understanding religious mores in terms of the rituals and their practices; it also means achieving scientific and technical knowledge related to both human society and the physical and biotic realms of our planet. A scientist in Islam can be theomorphic in the sense that he specializes in certain branches of science but at the same time possesses profound knowledge of the religion as well, a knowledge which provides a framework for the development of science in accordance with the principles of *tawhid* (Unity of God). For example, Aviccena was a physician and philosopher and yet was a good theologian.[51] In the context of man-environment interaction, the kind of knowledge that Islamic justice demands is knowledge of the effect of proposed action on the quality of the environment within which the community and its neighbors live. Any person who individually or collectively through his act of generating resource processes causes environmental disruption is considered guilty of violating the rules of justice and equity, and is consequently punished in accordance with the Quraan and the tradition of the Prophet (S.A.). Parenthetically, it may be noted that a modern version of such a law monitoring the impact of development is the "Environmental Impact Statement" mandated by the federal government of the United States under the National Environmental Policy Act of January 1970. EIS is a "mechanism to ensure that major projects or programs undergo comprehensive review prior to construction or implementation."[52] This law, however, has its own weaknesses, particularly from the standpoint of its application in a political system characterized by pressure groups.[53]

Summary and Conclusions

It can be asserted here that the ecological crisis faced by many developed and less-developed nations is in effect a moral crisis, and that it can be effectively dealt with by an Islamic ethics of decision-action processes. Unlike the materialist interpretation of development, the Islamic world view considers man, because of his theomorphic makeup, as ecologically dominant, but as an instrument of God's will to whom everything belongs. Man's freedom to convert resources and adjust spaces is controlled by justice, *taqwa*, and knowledge, including both theoretical and practical knowledge, which he is enjoined to observe, lest he become the sufferer. It is these variables, the guiding principles to the Islamic approach to environmental ethics, which provide the perceptual and behavior framework that helps us maintain the ecological equilibrium.

Man is constantly reminded by God that this world is only

a temporary abode for him, and that he must work here on this Earth in such a way as to be rewarded in the next world—his permanent place of residence. The caliph of the Islamic state is duty-bound to oversee human actions vis-à-vis the environment. He has the right to enforce laws and punish those whose actions are found to be blindly following the path of the maximization of benefits as well as those who ignore the ill effects that their actions are causing on the quality of the environment. Such people are disregarding the ethical spirit behind their right to subdue nature and benefit from natural resources. Indeed, the state processes in an Islamic state have to be subordinated to divine leadership, a kind of leadership which in the present circumstances can be possessed by a religious scholar or a council of such scholars well reputed in *taqwa*, for it is *taqwa* and knowledge which guarantee justice.

In particular, the findings of this paper can be of value to the Muslim world, where governments are embarking on various kinds of developmental programs. These programs need to be prepared and executed in such a way that the environmental quality of the areas involved is enriched rather than injured. As faithful adherents of Islam, they must work in accordance with the principles enunciated here, setting aside the idea of maximization of benefits without any regard for the maintenance of environmental balance. Our approach should be optimization of resources, and the alteration and modification of environmental features need to be properly managed in accordance with Islamic principles.

Notes

1. Peter Haggett, *Geography: A Modern Synthesis*, 2d ed. (New York: Harper and Row, 1975), p. 72; I. G. Simmons, *The Ecology of Natural Resources* (London: Edward Arnold), pp. 217–23.

2. Robert Kates, "Improving Societal Management of Technological Hazard" (Paper presented at the Workshop of the International Geographical Union Working Group on Environmental Perception, Ibadan, Nigeria, 1978), pp. 1–1a.

3. For details refer to the works like M. T. Farver and J. P. Milton, eds., *The Careless Technology: Ecology and International Development* (New York: Doubleday, 1972); R. F. Dasman et al., *Ecological Principles for Economic Development* (London: John Wiley and Sons, 1973); and I. H. Zaidi, "Land Use Hazards in an Arid Environment: The Case of Lower Indus Region," *Ecological Guidelines for the Use of Natural Resources in the Middle East and South West Asia* (Morges, Switzerland: International Union for Conservation of Nature and Natural Resources, 1976), pp. 38–59.

4. See for example C. O. Sauer, "The Agency of Man on Earth," in *Man's Role in Changing the Face of the Earth*, ed. W. L. Thomas, Jr. (Chicago: University of Chicago Press, 1956), pp. 49–60; M. W. Mikesell, "Geography as the Study of Environment: An Assessment of Some Old and New Commitments," in *Perspectives on Environment*, ed. I. R. Manners and M. W. Mikesell, Association of American Geographers, Commission on College Geography Publication no. 13 (Washington, D.C., 1974), pp. 1–23.

5. For an English translation of Al Quraan refer to M. Pickthal, *The Meaning of Glorious Koran* (London: George Allen and Unwin, 1930); see also S. V. M. Ahmad Ali, *Al Quraan: Translation and Notes* (Karachi: Sterling, 1964), s. (surah/chapter) 3, vs. (verses) 19, 84. S.A. and A.S. are benedictory formulas; the former is used specifically for Prophet Muhammad (S.A.), and in Arabic stands for variously, *Sallallaho Alayhe Wa Alehi Wa Sallam* or *Sallallah Alayhe-Wa-Sallam* ("May God send upon him and his descendants greetings and peace"); the latter stands for both singular and plural and means *Alaih-is-Salam* ("Peace be upon him [them]"), and is used for all other prophets and apostles and Shiite Imams.

6. S. H. Nasr, *An Introduction to Islamic Cosmological Doctrines* (Cambridge: Harvard University Press, Belknap Press, 1964), pp. 3–5.

7. Mikesell, "Geography," p. 17.
8. Simmons, *Ecology of Natural Resources* pp. 358–60; see J. Black, *The Dominion of Man* (Edinburgh: Edinburgh University Press, 1970); K. E. Boulding, "Environment and Economics" in W. W. Murdoch, ed., *Environment* (Stanford, Conn.: Sinauer, 1971), pp. 359–67; A. Toynbee, "The Religious Background of the Present Environmental Crisis," *International Journal of Environmental Studies* 3 (1972): 141–46; J. G. Bruhn, "The Ecological Crisis and World Ethics," *International Journal of Environmental Studies* 3 (1972): 43–47; see also R. J. Bennet and R. J. Chorley, *Environmental System, Philosophy, Analysis and Control* (London: Methuen, 1978), pp. 14–21.
9. Simmons, *Ecology of Natural Resources*, p. 369.
10. Lynn White, Jr., "The Historical Roots of Our Ecological Crisis," *Science* 155 (1967): 1205, 1206–7.
11. Toynbee, "Religious Background."
12. Yi Fu Tuan, "Discrepancies Between Environment Attitudes and Behavior: Examples from Europe and Canada," *Canadian Geographer* 13 (1968): 171–91.
13. White, "Historical Roots," pp. 1206–7.
14. See for example I. A. Matley, "Review of J. Passmore's *Man's Responsibility for Nature*," *Geographical Review* 65 (1975): 533–34.
15. Black, *Dominion of Man*.
16. Simmons, *Ecology of Natural Resources*, p. 29.
17. J. W. Bennet, *The Ecological Transition: Cultural Anthropology and Human Adaptation* (New York: Pergamon Press, 1976), pp. 94–95.
18. White, "Historical Roots," p. 1207.
19. Nasr, *Introduction*, p. 14.
20. M. Baqir Sadr, *Iqtisadona [Our Economics]*, Persian trans. M. Kazim Musawi, *Iqtisad-i-Ma* (Tehran: Intesharat Islami, 1971), pp. 20–28.
21. Ibid., p. 92.
22. Al Quraan, s.45, vs.12, 13; s.31, v. 20; s.14, vs.32, and 33.
23. Ibid., s.10, v.14.
24. Ibid., s.2, v.30.

25. H. M. Mehdi Pooya, *Fundamentals of Islam* (Karachi: Pakistan Herald Press, 1972), pp. 25–26.
26. For a good discussion see Nasr, *Introduction*, pp. 7–11.
27. Al Quraan, s.2, v.284.
28. Ibid., s.15, vs.19, 20.
29. Ibid., s.55, vs.8, 9, 10.
30. Ibid., s.41, v.53; s.45, v.12.
31. For an excellent discussion on *sign* see Yi Fu Tuan, "Signs and Metaphors," *Annals of the Association of American Geographers* 68 (1978): 263–72.
32. Ali Tehrani, *Iqtisad-i-Islami* [*Islamic Economics*] (Mashhad: Khorassan Press, 1974), pp. 209–11.
33. Nahjul Balagha, *Sermons, Letters, and Sayings of Hazrat Ali,* trans. M. Askari Jaferi (Karachi: Khorasan Islamic Centre, 1960), p. 287.
34. Ibid., p. 280.
35. *Grace* is defined as "to give out of sheer love without expecting any return," whereas "justice means 'He' keeps everything in its proper place and according to merit, so that the system should function as one harmonious unit representing the absolute unity of its Creator and Administrator. . . . Whatever He gives is out of sheer love but in accordance with the merit and appropriateness of the state of the receiver" (Pooya, *Fundamentals*, p. 113).
36. *Relative attribute* means any adjectival idea about God pertaining to some aspect of his action; Pooya, *Fundamentals*, p. 13.
37. Al Quraan, s. 21, vs. 101–7.
38. Ibid., s.68, v.4.
39. Nahjul Balagha, *Sermons*, p. 286.
40. Al Quraan, s.4, vs.58, 80.
41. Ibid., s.57, v.25.
42. Nahjul Balagha, *Sermons*, pp. 246–59.
43. For an elaborate discussion see Pooya, *Fundamentals*, pp. 20–22.
44. Al Quraan, s.7, v.26; see also s.49, v.13, s.5, v.2.
45. Ibid., s.2, v.247.

46. Ibid., s.2, vs.31–32.
47. Ibid., s.96, vs.1–5.
48. Ibid., s.37, v.36.
49. Ibid., s.17, v.85.
50. Ibid., s.20, v.114.
51. S. H. Nasr, *The Encounter of Man and Nature* (London: George Allen and Unwin, 1968), p. 97.
52. M. R. Grenberg, R. Anderson, and G. W. Page, *Environmental Impact Statements*, Resource Paper no. 78-3 (Washington, D.C.: Association of American Geographers, 1978), p. 2.
53. Ibid., pp. 15–29.

Sophie Jakowska

Roman Catholic Teaching and Environmental Ethics in Latin America

Although the preservation of the earth's riches has always been part of the teaching of the Roman Catholic church, only recently have questions about the just and rational management of natural resources become urgent. From mid-century onward, the church has increasingly addressed the problems of developing countries, Latin American nations among them. These problems are larger than environmental issues, and earliest attention was given to issues surrounding independence, neocolonialism, and social justice. More recently the concern of the church has been extended to environmental problems.

Using a series of four questions, I analyze the content and the effectiveness of the teaching of the Roman Catholic church, drawing on specific results and experience in the Dominican Republic, the first land in the New World to be claimed for the Spanish crown and the Catholic church by Columbus in 1492.

Can environmental ethics be derived from the religious beliefs of peoples, heirs to the Hispanic tradition, in Latin American countries that are facing an environmental crisis? Roman Catholic belief, like that of many Christian faiths, is drawn from the twin authorities of Bible and tradition. At least until the Renaissance, and the rise of modern science and technology, religion was the principal conceptual tool for the interpretation of nature. Several scholars have complained that the classical Christian teaching is anthropocentric and arrogant, slighting any real concern for nonhuman nature, and, hence, that the ecological crisis has religious roots.[1] Any solution to the problem would, therefore, involve some reformation of religious teaching.

Although millions of people profess to be Christians, relatively few are well informed enough on the actual contents of the Scriptures to appreciate the environmental implications of some texts. However, those who are familiar with the Scriptures know that the Bible never justifies indifference to the welfare of nonhuman creatures or arrogance toward what humans have been given by God in the natural world. Many of the principal roots of the environmental crisis lie elsewhere: perhaps in the mix of biblical Christianity and other cultural traditions, the mix of science and religion or their separation from each other, or, perhaps, in the liberties taken with the interpretation of the biblical texts.

Taken out of context, the Genesis "dominion" passages seem to ignore that humans were charged with stewardship over all the creation. The Psalmists[2] sing of the joys of the riches of a land as yet undegraded by human overuse. Psalm 8, a nature psalm, both praises God for his signs in the heavens and sets humans, under God, over the earth. The position asserts human superiority, but a conditioned superiority, involving responsibilities for appropriate use and care. In Psalm 23 uncontaminated nature is the ideal of peace: the Lord Shepherd leads his human sheep into verdant pastures and beside restful waters. In Psalm 50 God exclaims: "All the forest animals are already mine, . . . I know all the birds of the air, nothing moves in the field that does not belong to me."

Obviously, some "ecological awareness" existed among the Israelites; they knew their dependence upon the waters, the trees, the soil, the seasons. They used these natural metaphors as spiritual symbols: "Happy the man who . . . is like a tree that is planted by water streams, yielding its fruit in season, its leaves never fading" (Psalm 1). Nor should we forget that Roman Catholics have used Psalms and similar biblical passages regularly in their liturgy for quite a long time. They ought to be aware that the Israelites, as an agricultural people, used the fruits of their labor wisely and wasted nothing. Widows were allowed to glean wheat behind the reapers. The Hebrew festivals included holy days of thanksgiving for the spring and fall harvests.

The New Testament, compared with the Old, may appear less land oriented, but not less stewardship oriented. The goods of the earth are never despised, but are kept in their proper place in the kingdom where God's will is to be done on earth. Earthly possessions, about which Jesus has much to say, are not to be coveted or hoarded but charitably shared, used for the benefit of persons everywhere, with private property subordinated to common interests. All are brothers, all children of the same God, the Father. In this sense, Jesus has a lot to say about "natural resources." Additionally, Jesus when speaking about the kingdom draws many of his metaphors from the natural world: the kingdom grows like the harvest, the seed grows mysteriously, the Father cares for the sparrows, the lilies of the field put the glories of Solomon to shame. Jesus seems to see the same divine power evidenced in the natural world and in the coming kingdom.

In such biblical material there are ample resources for an environmental ethic. On the basis of the Scripture, it should be unthinkable for humans as rational beings to detract from the glory and service of God by knowingly contributing to the disappearance of any existing form of matter, living or nonliving, even though humans are permitted to share the earthly goods. Each form of matter is intrinsically valuable by the divine ordination: it glorifies its Creator. Rather than denying human superiority, this is quite consistent with holding that humans are a unique and privileged form of life, and that each created form deserves the human respect and protection.

Turning to the tradition of the church, we may take as an example the figure of Saint Francis of Assisi,[3] with his enormous appeal to the popular imagination. Saint Francis loved his fellow men, his fellow creatures, and counted the sun and the moon among his brothers and sisters. He preached to all God's creatures and sang canticles about God's marvelous creation. The year 1982 was the eighth centenary of his birth. Saint Francis was more influential in shaping the mood of the Hispanic church than is often realized, and perhaps we can now see him as the forerunner of the cosmic vision of all humankind, in harmony with all things created, on the way toward perfection far beyond the evolutionary level achieved to date.

In her "Golden Century" Spain was firmly bound with religion,[4] and mysticism was said to be "inborn in Spain's character." There was a close relation between Spanish mysticism and nature, as shown in the "cosmic feeling" of writers such as Saint Theresa of Avila, who frequently used references to nature.[5] The religious orders that came to the New World were influenced by mysticism, but the church at the time of the discovery cannot be said to have been particularly concerned with the protection of nature or the conservation of Earth's resources for the benefit of all peoples. The first missionaries to arrive were of the Dominican Order of Preachers[6]; they were heirs both to Aristotelian Thomism and to the view of the importance of nature held by Saint Augustine, but they became above all champions of human rights. Perhaps the Franciscans and the Jesuits, who came after them, had a greater influence on the relation of men with nature: the Jesuits' founder, Saint Ignatius Loyola,[7] viewed the world in a somewhat Franciscan tradition, seeing God in all things.

These religious traditions were applied in the New World with mixed effects. For the Europeans of 1492, the New World was only a temporary home for which there was no need to care. The conquistadors, nevertheless, were products of their time and society. It is interesting that the first (and only) conservation measure of that time was the royal ordinance ("Real Cedula") of the Emperor Charles V (1539), which obliged the colonizers to plant trees around villages so that wood for fuel would be available.[8] There is no indication how effectively this ordinance was applied.

In this century, however, environmental issues have become extremely serious in countries of the Third World. These nations may be robbed forever of their natural heritage, repeating mistakes made by the more advanced countries, being urged to do so by those countries seeking to expand their influence. It might first seem that there is little in the Hispanic-Catholic past in Latin America which will have very much power in addressing the ecological crisis. Although it is true that the roots are there in the biblical tradition and that the church has always been committed, if in theory more than in practice, to a stewardship of all resources, the church itself had no control over the resulting environmental problems that plague Latin America today. However, people with the pluralistic cultural heritage of Hispanic Catholicism are now being reached so that the message of nature's stewardship may be translated into practice before it is too late.

Does the Roman Catholic church today offer clear guidelines as to the human use of natural resources? The Catholic church did not move directly into environmental ethic in this century, but rather has gradually evolved more and more toward environmental concerns as a result of its growing concern for social justice. Although some may say its teaching is more resource oriented, a number of significant documents have environmental implications and represent clear guidelines to the members of the Catholic church.

For easier reference these documents are discussed as four units: (1) early documents with primarily social concern, (2) environmental concerns of Pope Paul VI, (3) environmental concerns since Paul VI, and (4) documents specific for Latin America and/or the Dominican Republic. Each of these documents ought to be studied in detail by those doctrinally inclined; for those concerned with environmental ethics, the highlights of their contents will suffice to appreciate the trends and the emphasis expressed in each.

Rerum Novarum, promulgated by Leo XIII in 1891, is the first declaration of the social implications of Christian faith. It starts the "environmental trend," pointing out that earthly goods are here for all to share. Forty years later, Pius XI published the encyclical *Quadragesimo Anno*, in which the term *social justice* was used for the first time in a pontifical document; the need for a fair distribution of natural resources among all men and for limiting private property was also stressed.

Pius XII in his radio message for Christmas 1953 expressed the preoccupation with the alienating effects of technology, though admitting that it gave man a greater dominion over the material world and much of the progress that is beneficial. Pope John XXIII in *Mater et Magistra* (1959) fully extended the scope of social doctrine to the question of the common good on national, international, and global levels. In his encyclical *Pacem in Terris* (1963) he appealed to all to strive for peace based on truth, justice, love, and freedom, which are essential for sharing natural resources.

A more specific environmental turn begins with Pope Paul VI, who on the eve of the closing session of Vatican II promulgated the pastoral letter *Gaudium et Spes* (1965). In it Paul VI reiterates the fundamental truth that Man, created in the image of God, was placed in the center of creation to contemplate it and to rule the earth (no. 34). Man, however, must care for all creation through work (no. 67). All earthly goods are meant to be shared in a just and equitable way so that men can live with dignity and grow physically and spiritually (no. 69). This letter is also critical of the abuses of private property, when it may become a menace to the common good. Land not in use can, therefore, be rightfully occupied to be cultivated, and those who block the use of such land or water for its development are not acting rightfully.

This papal recommendation, from the vantage point of hindsight, could be incorrectly interpreted and result in environmentally adverse acts. For example, it might seem to justify the invasion of national parks or forest reserves by landless, nomadic peasants who burn or otherwise clear the forest, converting it into land of doubtful productivity. In a country like the Dominican Republic, such action is referred to as "cleaning" (*limpiar*) a forest, a term with a positive connotation, which in fact describes an ecologically negative act. The papal recommendation could also exert pressure on owners of virgin lands of primary ecological importance, such as tropical and subtropical rain forests, to parcel out the land for the agrarian reform. This, however, goes against the intentions of this document, since, as shown in a test case in South America a few years ago, virgin forests are of such regional, national, and international importance that these larger claims override local needs.

In the encyclical *Populorum Progressio* (1967) Paul VI, while focusing on the needs of the poor in less developed nations, takes note of the unequal distribution of natural resources among the nations and of the environmental crisis. However, it is in the apostolic letter to Cardinal Mauricio Roi, known as *Octogesima Adveniens* (1971), written on the occasion of the eightieth anniversary of *Rerum Novarum*, that Paul VI takes up the ecological challenge. He questions the supposed advantages of industrial society and of consumer culture, which threaten the quality of human life. He goes on to point out how these human activities are beginning to cause dramatic and unexpected changes in the natural order. Because of the irrational exploitation of nature, man is now in danger of destroying the earth and becoming victim of this degradation. In the encyclical *Evangelii Nuntiandi* (1975) lay people are given a specific responsibility for building the temporal society, and ecology is presented as a moral issue. In an apostolic exhortation published the same year under the title *Gaudete in Domino*, Pope Paul VI wishes all men to share God's joy in his creation, since it is meant to be a source of joy for men in itself, unless, of course, it becomes hopelessly damaged, something that is beyond the power of the church to control.

A very strong stand on environmental matters is taken by Paul VI on the occasion of the fifth World Environment Day in 1977, in a message to the United Nations entitled "Preserving and Improving the Environment for the Benefit of Man." He states that the environment in which we live is essentially good, as the environment in which we were placed to live out our calling in solidarity with each other. According to the pope, before man fell into sin, the world was a paradise: beautiful, intact, harmonious nature. But nature was unbalanced by man who rebelled against God. Now nature rebels against man. By reconciling humans with God the Father, and with each other, Christ started the rec-

onciliation of man with nature. The fulfillment of the Kingdom of God includes an ecological dimension: nature will
regain the lost balance and will participate in the liberation
of all God's children. It is pointed out that the Christian vision of ecology is based on such texts as Romans 8, Ephe-
sians 1, Colossians 4, and Revelation 21–22, which speak of
a freedom of the children of God, liberated by grace which
mysteriously also liberates nature, the new heaven and the
new earth revealing their splendor to God himself. All creation must return to the resurrected Christ, to be delivered
to the Father, when God will be all in all things.

Pope John Paul II is known from his prepontifical days for
his concern for modern man's capacity to understand and to
fulfill the biblical message of Genesis: man has reached the
moon on the strength of his intelligence, yet he is apt to
destroy his environment (1976).[9] In his first encyclical, *Re-
demptor Hominis* (1979), he asserts the priority of ethics
over technology, persons over things, and spirit over matter.
But he adds that humans at times seem unaware of their
natural environment except for consumer purposes. Yet it
was the Creator's will that men confront their environment
not just as "exploiters" and "destroyers," but as intelligent
and noble "keepers." He finds a number of environmental
problems alarming: pollution, the progressive deterioration
of material and energy resources, our uncontrolled technology, and our endangered geophysical environment. He
concludes that the fair and just exploitation of the earth requires rational and honest planning.

Laborem Exercens (1981) continues these themes with
the ways in which people are to work and plan in order to
exercise their prerogative of ruling the earth. There is a clear
indication of the awareness that our natural heritage is limited, unacceptably contaminated, and in danger of being destroyed by the use of nuclear weapons.

The "Peace Document," delivered by John Paul II on the

fifteenth World Peace Day in 1982, includes the idea that ecological damage is the cause of human conflicts. Natural resources are a gift of God entrusted to man, to administer and to develop in the service of all. Through science and technology man must liberate nature's potential for the benefit of all mankind. In the same year, the pope also stressed our responsibility for the environment using Saint Francis of Assisi as a model on the occasion of the eight hundredth anniversary of his birth, a date coinciding with National Ecology Day in Italy. We cannot, he writes, continue as predators, destroying what was provided through God's wisdom; we must respect nature in order to preserve a suitable environment for future generations. And finally in his address at the symposium "Towards the Year 2000," John Paul II called for a new economic system that will assure human dignity and a just distribution of the natural resources, which are God's property.

According to the pope, the defense of nature and of the environment is part of the Maker's plan of redemption. Life on earth cannot have its fullest Christian meaning if there is destruction of the natural components of life on this marvelous and favored planet, on which God has willed himself, in his Son, to share the splendid planetary and human adventure.

With these spiritual and temporal considerations as a background, and the reality of life in their area, the Episcopal Conference of Latin America (CELAM) has striven, since Medellín in 1968, to improve the human environment and has inspired much ecologically positive thought and action.[10] Nevertheless, a more concrete plan for the responsible use of resources was developed in the document produced by a group of three hundred bishops, priests, and laymen during a conference held in Puebla, Mexico, in early 1979, inaugurated by John Paul II.[11]

The Puebla document deals principally with Latin American reality in terms of its cultural, economic, political, demographic, and ecclesiastical aspects. It proposes a plan for church action in Latin America during the next ten years. It is significant that a number of paragraphs refer specifically to ecological issues; these are summarized below and identified by number, as in the Spanish original.[12]

Dangers are foreseen from pressures resulting from accelerated demographic growth (no. 127) and from the frustrations and tensions produced by contrasts between those living in opulence and those in extreme poverty (no. 138). If these trends do not change, the document concludes, man's relation with nature will continue to deteriorate as a result of the irrational exploitation of natural resources and environmental pollution which endangers both man and the ecological balance (no. 139).

The use and the transformation of natural resources must be accomplished through a just and brotherly lordship of man over the world, and with respect for ecology (no. 327). Earth's goods, by their origin and nature, according to the will of the Creator, are meant to serve effectively for the use and benefit of all men and all nations (no. 492). Yet uncontrolled industrialization and alarming urban growth leads to the depletion of these natural resources and to environmental pollution (no. 496). Hence, it is necessary to preserve the natural resources created by God for all men, in order to transmit them to the future generations as an enriching heritage (no. 1236).

Scientists, technicians, and builders of our technological society can help to investigate the enigmas of the universe and to manage the earth (no. 1240). The sovereignty of nations must take precedence over multinational enterprises in the use and control of the natural resources (no. 1264).

It can be easily seen that the ideas expressed in the previous church documents found their way to serve in a more practical manner as guidelines for action in Latin America. The inclusion of so many ecological issues in the Puebla document marks a trend toward increasing concern on the part of the church for the quality of life, in a very integrated sense. Bigó and Bastos de Avila (1981),[13] in a publication sponsored by CELAM, provide an overview of the environmental problems in Latin America, intended for the benefit of church personnel. Until about eighteen years ago, only a few isolated experts were aware of the depletion of natural resources and of environmental pollution brought about by modern industrial technology. Today the degradation of biosystems (marine fisheries, forest resources, soils, and water reserves) is recognized as being extremely alarming. No one knows how much longer these conditions can continue without affecting human survival. The excessive extraction of mineral resources (oil, coal, natural gas) only adds to this concern. Some agricultural practices used today damage the soil irreversibly, and the urgent needs of the poor transform forests into deserts, with only a short-term gain. Nuclear energy and chemical pollution may soon make it impossible to use air, water, and soil.

The National Episcopal Conference of Brazil in 1979 responded to the ecological challenge with ten statements on environmental ethics, as part of the Brotherhood Campaign, under the title "To Preserve What Belongs to All Men":[14]

1. The world, with its natural resources, is a mirror which reflects the beauty and goodness of God. We should avoid anything that might darken this reflection and disfigure the gift that God in his infinite love has prepared for his children.

2. We should contribute to the beauty of the world, so that we may see flowers opening and stars shining, so that we may hear the song of the birds and the laughter of children, all a sign that God's blessing has not as yet left our earth.

3. God's providence has endowed the earth with the necessary resources to guarantee the life of all persons. We

should avoid any forms of waste and unnecessary consumption, remembering that our irrational use of goods deprives a brother of the necessities for subsistence.

4. God destined the earth and all its resources for the freedom and advancement of all persons, not for the exclusive benefit of some groups or nations. We should use this freedom responsibly, not to destroy but to build a world where all may live as brothers.

5. Through work, destined to provide the maintenance of all, humans must discover each other as brothers and complete the creative work of God. In this work we should try not to disturb but rather to enhance the admirable balance of nature that makes possible the continuity of life.

6. The creation of conditions that will improve the quality of life of our brothers depends on ourselves. We must not contribute to the increasing contamination which will make life on Earth intolerable. The most detestable form of contamination is the poverty of one's brothers, deprived through injustice.

7. Humans were created to use natural resources in a way necessary for their fulfillment as sons of God. We should free ourselves of the obsessive preoccupation to have more all the time, as this brings oppression to others and makes us slaves to material things.

8. Improper use of the goods that God has offered us is a sin, since it turns us away from the purpose for which we were created. In this sense, sin is a profaning of nature and its resources. Nobody who defiles the gifts of God can go unpunished.

9. We should look for new ways to fulfill our dignity as humans and sons of God independently of worries about accumulating more property and resources. We must learn to be more through having less.

10. We must remember that what gives meaning to life is more important than life itself.

The church has already been instrumental in creating an ecological awareness in Latin America and in other countries with a Catholic heritage. But in view of the urgency of environmental issues, it would be worthwhile to increase the activities of church-related institutions and organizations and to make greater use of the expertise of the members of the Pontifical Academy of Sciences with regard to environmental pollution, the prevention of extinction among endangered species, the application of the principles of the World Strategy for Survival (IUCN),[15] and the development of an environmental code of ethics.

Progress has already been made on the regional level. In the Dominican Republic the Episcopal Conference has been responding to the ecological challenge since about 1980, without counting the individual declarations of the bishops. Two pastoral letters published in 1982, and one in 1983, carry ecological implications. A pastoral letter on environmental issues was in 1984 being prepared. These documents faithfully reflect the stand of the church and already serve as a means for communication with the faithful and (as shown by a recent event) also as an instrument for ecologically positive action.

Can the church's environmental teachings be transmitted effectively to the masses in order to alleviate environmental degradation? The nature and structure of the Catholic church cannot be explained in simple sociological and historical terms. According to Vatican II,[16] the church describes itself as both human and divine, made up of visible and invisible elements, and given to both action and contemplation. It is governed by the Code of Canon Law,[17] recently revised and in effect since November 1983, which sets the norms in practically every aspect of religious life for the orderly and unified functioning of the centralized and peripheral institutions.

The church assumes the role of the supreme teacher, and Catholics everywhere accept the authority of the pope who, as successor of Saint Peter (with the bishops, as successors of the Apostles), governs the church, and whose decisions are irrevocable. As teacher, the pope is considered infallible when he speaks *urbi et orbi* in matters of faith and morals. The bishops, although not considered infallible, have the obligation to channel the teaching down to the pastors and to the faithful.

The papal documents and the pastoral letters of the bishops represent the actualized teaching of the church, the reason why those with environmental implications were described in such detail. The way in which this teaching can be transmitted and become effective depends greatly on the existing channels for communication between church leaders and the Catholics, as well as on the ability to translate this teaching into a simpler language.

In Latin America people call themselves Catholics principally because they were so baptized. Some are the "evangelized" minority (church leaders and religiously enlightened persons); but for the majority, the Catholic religion may be the residue of colonial Christendom (native Indians, mestizos, and Creoles), or of European Christianity (European immigrants).[18] There is an obvious need for a continued evangelization of the masses in Latin America before any serious de-Christianization takes place. This evangelization process could also include the essential ecological precepts and help men become reconciled not only with God and their fellow men, but with nature as well. Perhaps the path of religion might accomplish the change of hearts and of minds among those for whom arguments from science and technology have no appeal, especially those who cannot as yet afford the luxury of concern.[19]

In Latin America today, CELAM may already be considered an ally of the environmental movement. Founded in Rio de

Janeiro in 1955, it was rather well represented numerically at the Second Vatican Council, it was reorganized in accordance with the new conciliar ideas, and it became the first group to develop the concept of episcopal collegiality in a permanent and organic way. It produced significant guidelines in Medellín and in Puebla, taking a stand against underdevelopment and in favor of the poor. It encouraged the creation of new lay institutions and a more active participation of lay persons in church affairs. None of its specialized departments, however, seems specifically oriented toward environmental matters or environmental ethics.

On the national level CELAM is complemented by the National Conferences of Bishops, and it reaches the clergy and the laity through pastoral letters that are communicated at parish and community level, and through the communications media and the Catholic press.

Members of the religious orders in Latin America are organized into CLAR (Latin American Confederation of Religions), with their national federations. They have considerable influence on people at the parish and community level as well as on the youth through the direct involvement of priests, brothers, and sisters of various religious congregations in educational institutions and youth organizations. Ecological issues have been incorporated in many educational activities, especially in the education of rural youth.

An important role in evangelization and in the environmental movement is being assumed by ecclesiastical base communities (Comunidad Eclesial de Base, or CEB), a phenomenon typical of Latin America. Begun after Medellín and promoted in the encyclical *Evangelii Nuntiandi* of Paul VI, they represent small rural and urban groups, not always parish related, united in their faith for community worship, catechesis, and community action. The capacity of such groups for ecologically positive action for human development and for the improvement of the quality of life cannot be underestimated. Their number in a country may be a better measure of true Catholic spirit than any statistics dealing with the number of baptized members of the church.

In the highly pluralistic Latin American church, CEB may permit the genuine expression, within each cultural and socioeconomic group, of the aspirations of the people united under God. Their significance becomes even more apparent when we consider statistics for particular countries, for example, the Dominican Republic in 1981–82. The country, with an estimated population of 5,570,000 people, is divided into eight dioceses with twelve bishops (two retired, one of them a cardinal). It has 207 parishes, urban and rural, with a total of 473 priests, 358 of whom belong to twenty-three different religious groups. In addition, 1,103 women in forty-four religious orders and seven secular institutes are active in the Dominican Republic.

In view of the relatively small number of priests per capita, it is significant that the Dominican Republic has almost a thousand ecclesiastical base communities. Leadership among laymen is nurtured in centers for social promotion and centers for rural promotion, located in dioceses, which offer special courses, usually two to three days long, with each center providing accomodations for up to one hundred persons per course. These are complemented by centers for catechesis, cultural centers, and mothers' clubs.

Youth ministry is a great but still untapped source of environmental action and education. During recent years the ministry has grown spiritually and increased in social awareness, and now consists of many organizations, some with Salesian or Jesuit advisers.

Some environmental teaching starts early in the Dominican Republic. In accordance with the religious study program designed by Virginia Laporte, O.S.U., for the Catechistic Institute Fray Ramon Pané, ecological concepts are introduced to first-grade pupils (and their teachers) in five of fifteen broader themes, presenting water, sun, plants, animals, people, and one's own potential as God's gifts. The institute plans to add more environmental principles to the religious teaching for the higher levels in the future.

An excellent instrument for the diffusion of the church's teaching has been produced by Ramon De La Rosa, a clergyman who collaborated in the writing of the Puebla document. His *Puebla para el Pueblo* (Puebla for People) is a series of pamphlets written in a clear and humorous manner, accompanied by comic-book-style line drawings, and faithful to the text on which they are based. The pamphlets are used by ecclesiastical base communities and in various courses, since they are inexpensive and accessible to people with little formal education. Three versions exist: "En Dibujos"[20] for individual and group study, "En Asambleas"[21] for meetings, with an agenda and programs of related activities, and "En Celebraciones"[22] meant for community worship, with suggestions for individual and group expression through liturgy. Destruction of natural resources, with a stress on deforestation, is included in the texts. This approach is so good that the environmental issues presented in the Puebla document would probably benefit from an even more extensive treatment in the format of *Puebla para el Pueblo*.

Two additional resources are the Catholic press and Catholic radio stations, which contribute to social awareness, fight illiteracy, and promote education. They regularly disseminate the pastoral messages that deal with environment or other matters. In the Dominican Republic, Radio Santa Maria in La Vega pioneered a home study program in rural areas, from which thousands have received a basic education. This station seems perfectly qualified to impart instruction that could bring about an essential change in attitudes toward nature among Dominicans. Other radio stations are located in the southwest, near the Haitian frontier, and in the east, with the newest in the Archdiocese of Santo Domingo, all serving the Catholic population.

The Catholic press in the Dominican Republic includes *Amigo del Hogar*, a monthly with a circulation of over ten thousand, *Sembrador Mañanero*, with considerable appeal to farmers, and the weekly *El Camino*, which shows considerable environmental concern. As compared with some other countries in Latin America, the Catholic press here is relatively young.

One should also not forget charitable organizations such as CARITAS, which have an opportunity to promote environmentally oriented projects together with their educational and health programs.

The Latin American church continues to face manpower shortages: as compared with countries such as the United States, the ratio of priests to faithful is very low. Thus, some of the teaching that was formerly relegated to the clergy must be accomplished by the laity. On the other hand, the existing channels of communication between the church leaders and the people of Latin America appear suitable for the implementation of environment-related church doctrine, especially in view of the increased commitment of the episcopal conference and of the laity to human development projects with ecological implications. All these programs might benefit from a closer collaboration with the Pontifical Academy of Sciences, an important body of experts who might thereby develop greater interest in the environmental needs of this part of the world.

People of Latin America do not live in a religiously dominated culture, but they do live in a culture of poverty in which the Catholic church is already playing a liberating role. Man is the primary concern of the church and it is for man's sake that the church is trying to transmit its ecological tenets and continues to reiterate the warnings against human activities that would impair the quality of the world we live in and cause the destruction of the human race. But in order that these efforts may be effective, there is perhaps a need to develop international, national, and local programs directed at a reconciliation of man with nature, which is spiritually strong, theologically well grounded, and capable of generating more than temporal leadership in church-inspired ecologically positive action. We need a movement leading toward an environmental religious culture.

Is there evidence that something ecologically positive is being accomplished through church-inspired action in a developing country such as the Dominican Republic? Tracing the roots for his compatriots' lack of concern for the natural resources in the Dominican Republic, Vega (1978) pointed out that during the first three centuries of colonization the laws relating to land and agriculture (1591 and 1631) were meant to exploit, never to conserve. Common pastures and free-grazing cattle destroyed forests. Export of mahogany, oak, and ebony became the chief source of government income, and cutting down trees along the river banks provided the easiest way of transportation. The pattern of exploitation continued into the first years of independence.

Nature protection started with the law of 1884, which required that 5 percent of a forest being converted to arable land be preserved uncut and prohibited the cutting of trees near water sources. Law no. 944 of 1928 permitted the establishment of forest reserves on all state property, especially near river sources. The first national park was founded soon afterward. During Trujillo's dictatorship the country signed the first international treaty on nature protection, but at the same time high-powered sawmills were installed, and private abuse of public forests remained the rule. Starting in 1962, however, three important laws were passed: Law no. 5852 (*Dominio de las Aguas Terrestres*), Law no. 5856 (*Ley*

Forestal), and Law no. 5914 (*Ley de Pesca*). These measures were designed to protect water resources, forests, and wild-life.

While the existing laws are theoretically adequate for the protection of flora and fauna, they are difficult to enforce, since many people refuse to obey them; besides, they are not uniformly and justly applied. A change in the attitude toward nature is therefore urgently needed. Given these difficulties, it is remarkable that a small rural parish in San José de Ocoa (Archdiocese of Santo Domingo) should be singled out in the environmental profile of the Dominican Republic[23] as a community that shows exceptional cooperation in soil conservation, the planting of fruit trees, and the construction of channel terraces, small sedimentation dams, and other antierosion projects.

The Association for the Development of San José de Ocoa, started in 1962 and incorporated in 1968,[24] is a genuine church-inspired movement, in a place where soil and water resources were sorely depleted and where peasants with little or no land represent 74 percent of the population. The movement, which has been under the spiritual guidance of Father Luis Quinn for almost twenty years, depends on people who are highly motivated to build their own destiny and who aim to accomplish deep and positive changes in their society, without regard for personal gain or political interests. They are convinced that the country does have sufficient natural and economic resources to build a better life for all Dominicans, and that the people must help themselves.[25]

Recently the movement engaged the help of students from two universities to do a geological survey necessary for the reconstruction of a canal. In 1981, at the First Seminar on Socioeconomic Reality in San José de Ocoa, they made a number of important recommendations on environmental protection.[26] They also carry on environmental education in radio talks, lectures on a technical level, and courses for local farmers.

Action, education, and religion are closely united in San Jose de Ocoa, where, in preparation for a feast of Our Lady of Altagracia, their patron, nine consecutive evenings were dedicated to reflection on the ecological challenge of the Ocoa community, with massive attendance and participation in liturgies oriented toward the reconciliation of men with nature. Early in 1984, soon after this religious-ecological event, the Association for the Development hosted an international symposium-workshop under the joint auspices with CODEL (Coordination in Development), an ecumenical organization dealing with human improvement projects. Today, with many struggles still ahead, the Ocoa community projects itself internationally as a church-inspired, ecologically positive program of proven vitality.

Another example of a church-inspired project in the Dominican Republic, which has developed into a major government ecological program, is Plan Sierra,[27] described in an environmental profile as "one of two major plans existing in the Dominican Republic which have a reforestation component." Plan Sierra was actually a brainchild of Monsignor Roque Adames,[28] bishop of Santiago and the third rector of the Catholic University (Universidad Católica Madre y Maestra or UCMM). During his pastoral visits to the parishes of his diocese in 1967, the bishop was shocked by the ongoing deforestation and destruction of the land, not unlike that which had already converted neighboring Haiti, once rich, into an ecological disaster area. He took up the challenge at no little risk of being criticized as a pastor of trees rather than a pastor of souls.

Plan Sierra, started modestly on a diocesan basis, achieved a national and international status by 1978, and in March 1979 received 800,000 pesos in government funding. The projects encompass the area known as Cibao, remarkable for its fertile lowlands, as well as the mountain regions of San José de Las Matas and Jánico in Santiago province, and Monción in the province of Santiago Rodriguez. The philosophy of Plan Sierra is to develop natural resources while protecting the environment. Projects focus on agricultural production for export, development of animal husbandry and pastures, reforestation (especially with *Pinus caribaea*), technological training, and health and social services.

The approaches for which Plan Sierra is being praised are founded in the social doctrine of the Catholic church, and on the church's teaching on human responsibility for the environment. The way both the San José de Ocoa and Plan Sierra projects are working out may indicate that environmental ethics based on the teaching of the church is more reliable than ethics based on scientific and technological arguments. The direct involvement of Catholics in major community action, moreover, shows how work transforms and liberates the potential that the Creator placed on earth for the needs of all men.

There is a need for a text on environmental culture for the clergy and for people preparing for the priesthood or other forms of service in the church. The book *Fé cristiana y compromiso social* ("Christian Faith and Social Commitment"), published in 1981 under the auspices of CELAM, partly fills this need: it takes up ecological destruction, ecological crisis, and ecological problems in the thought of Paul VI and of John Paul II, and provides an ethical orientation as to man's relation with nature and the question of ecological balance.

Last but not least in importance, as church-inspired ecologically positive action, is the stand taken by the bishop of Barahona, Monsignor Fabio Mamerto Rivas Santos, who expressed opposition to a plan to store wastes of a doubtful nature in a landfill near Oviedo. His arguments (and those of his advisory group), as well as the protests of conservation-minded citizens, helped reverse what was practically a decision of the government.

Latin America is notorious for its use of pharmaceutical, agrochemical, and other products that have been taken off the market as unsafe in the more advanced countries. The fact that a bishop's circular letter and popular support could achieve ecologically positive results in 1983 implies that there is some degree of environmental awareness and that perhaps the Dominican Republic may soon be able to afford the luxury of concern for its natural national heritage.

Conclusion

The pressure of environmental problems affecting all nations has broken the barrier of silence on the religious aspects of human actions, formerly an unpopular topic among academicians, scientists, and professionals in general. Today we are coming to realize that perhaps by listening to our respective religious leaders concerning environmental issues, we shall jointly discover the ecumenical path toward the solution of the environmental problems that we are so earnestly seeking with the help of science and technology.

The members of the Catholic church do not always obey the precepts of their faith, and at times they are not sufficiently mature to understand them, but perhaps problems associated with the diminishing resources of our plundered planet will eventually bring them around to heed the teaching on stewardship. It is to be hoped that Catholics in Latin America will soon reach a state of ecological awareness, that they will embrace environmental ethics and make use of all the means at their disposal in order to be effective as defenders of nature in their communities. Fortunately, the church in Latin America is ecologically aware and committed to the

cause of the environment. It provides the necessary guidelines and is open to collaboration in ecumenical projects.

Humankind's capacity to understand God's plan for man
in the universe is far greater than ever before. It is our duty
to recognize this plan.[29]

Notes

1. Lynn White, Jr., "The Historical Roots of Ecological Crisis,"
   Science 155 (1967): 1205.
2. Psalms cited according to *The Jerusalem Bible* (Garden City,
   N.Y.: Doubleday, 1966).
3. José Antonio Guerra, *San Francisco de Asis: Escritos, Biog-
   rafías, Documentos de la Epoca* (Madrid: La Editorial Catolica,
   1978).
4. R. Trevor Davies, *The Golden Century of Spain 1501–1621*
   (New York: Harper and Row, 1937).
5. E. Allison Peers, *Spanish Mysticism* (London: Methuen, 1924).
6. Fray Pedro de Córdoba, Fray Bartolomé de las Casas, Fray Antonio de Montesinos, and other members of the Order of
   Preachers started arriving on Hispaniola in 1510. The first university of the New World was founded with the papal bull *In
   apostolatus culmine,* issued by Paul III in 1538. The first teachers in the university named after St. Thomas Aquinas were
   members of the Order of Preachers (Dominicans).
7. Ignacio Iparraguirre S.I. and Candido de Dalmases S.I., *San Ignacio de Loyola: Obras Completas* (Madrid: La Editorial
   Catolica, 1982).
8. Wenceslao Vega B., *La Conservacion Ambiental y la Ley,* Documentos de Trabajo, Coloquio Internacional sobre la Práctica de
   la Conservacion Santo Domingo, CIBIMA, UASD, 1978.
9. Karol Wojtyla, *Segno di Contraddizione* (Milano: Universita
   Cattolica del Sacro Cuore, 1976).
10. CELAM, "The Church in the Present-Day Transformation of
    Latin America in the Light of the Council," Medellín, 1968.

11. CELAM, "Puebla: La Evangelizacion en el Presente y en el Futuro de America Latina," III Conferencia General del Episcopado Latinoamericano Amigo del Hogar, Santo Domingo, 1979.

12. Sophie Jakowska, "El Documento de Puebla y los Bienes de la Tierra: Reflexiones en ocasion del Día Mundial del Ambiente, 1980," circular no. 6, Arzobispado de Santo Domingo, 15 May 1980; reprinted in *Amigo del Hogar* 30 (1980): 22–23.

13. Pierre Bigó, S. J., and Fernando Bastos de Avila, S. J., *Fé Cristiana y Compromiso Social: Elementos para una Reflexion sobre América Latina a la Luz de la Doctrina Social de la Iglesia* (Lima: CELAM, 1981).

14. Conferencia Episcopal de Brasil, "Preservar lo que es de Todos" Campaña de Fraternidad de la CNBB, 1979.

15. International Union for the Conservation of Nature and Natural Resources, "Estrategia Mundial para la Conservacion," Gland, Switzerland, 1980.

16. Enrique Rondet, *Vaticano II: El Concilio de la Nueva Era* (Bilbao: Desclée de Brouwer, 1970).

17. *Codigo de Derecho Canonico,* Edicion Bilingue Comentada (Madrid: La Editorial Catolica, 1983).

18. Enrique Dussel, *A History of the Church in Latin America: Colonialism to Liberation* (Grand Rapids, Mich.: William B. Eerdmans, 1981).

19. Robert M. Alison, "The Earliest Traces of a Conservation Conscience, *Natural History* 90 (1981): 73–77.

20. Ramon De La Rosa et al., *Puebla para el Pueblo, en Dibujos,* nos. 1 and 2 (Santo Domingo: Amigo del Hogar, 1980).

21. Ramon De La Rosa et al., *Puebla para el Pueblo, en Asambleas,* nos. 1 and 2 (Santo Domingo: Amigo del Hogar, 1981).

22. Jaime Reynes, *Puebla para el Pueblo, en Celebraciones,* nos. 1 and 2 (Santo Domingo: Amigo del Hogar, 1981).

23. Gary Harshorn et al., *The Dominican Republic, Country, Environmental Profile: A Field Study,* (McLean, Va.: JRB Associates, 1981).

24. Santa Baez, Tomás Isa, Manuel Martinez, Diosteria Baez, and Luis José Quinn. "Exposición de la Asociacion para el Desarrollo de San José de Ocoa," Actividades Adicionales, 1981.

25. Informe General de las Principales Actividades Realizadas en el

Periodo Octubre 1980–Octubre 1981, Proyecto Integrado de Conservacion de Suelo (with the joint participation of the Secretaria de Estado de Agricultura, Proyecto Dominico-Aleman Santa Cruz, Direccion Forestal, and the Junta de Desarrollo, Misereor).

26. Luis José Quinn, "Comentario a la Ponencia: Manejo de Recursos Naturales en San Jose de Ocoa, Asociacion de Estudiantes Universitarios Ocoenos (AEUO), 1981.

27. Secretaria de Estado de Agricultura, Departamento de Planificacion, "Plan de Desarrollo La Sierra," Santo Domingo, May 1978.

28. Francisco José Arnáiz, S.J., "Plan Sierra, Orgullo y Ejemplo," Suplemento Listín Diario, 11 February 1984.

29. See Francisco José Arnáiz, S.J., "El Plan del Padre," Suplemento Listín Diario, 22 February 1986.

The author gratefully acknowledges the editorial assistance of Eugene C. Hargrove and Holmes Rolston, III. She thanks Fco. José Arnáiz, S.J., and Walenty Debski, S. D. B., for orientation and encouragement, Monsignor Roque Adames and Father Luis Quinn for information on their projects, and Luis Rosariom S. D. B., and Virginia Laporte, O. S. U., for the critical reading of an earlier draft of the paper.

Robert H. Ayers

Christian Realism and Environmental Ethics

D uring the last decade a great deal has been written concerning the implications to be found in Christian theology for our present ecological crisis. Some of it has been amazingly ill-informed and naïve, as when, for example, the Berkeley Ecological Revolutionary Organization listed the ancient Gnostics as among those who have been ecologically enlightened.[1] Of course, just the opposite is the case, since the Gnostics held that while the realm of the spirit is good, the realm of the physical is evil. Although most persons concerned with environmental issues are generally better informed and refrain from making such extreme statements, there are some who claim that the Judeo-Christian tradition has been a major contributor to our ecological crisis.

Perhaps the most famous of those who have argued that the Judeo-Christian tradition is a culprit is the historian Lynn White, Jr. In a well-known and widely quoted article, "The Historical Roots of our Ecological Crisis,"[2] White goes so far as to speak of the "orthodox Christian arrogance toward nature,"[3] an arrogance which he thinks has its foundation in the biblical myths of creation. This perspective, he claims, provided the major motivation for the West's technological despoiling of the environment, and as a result, the

Judeo-Christian tradition "bears a huge burden of guilt"[4] for our ecological crisis.

White's thesis has been challenged along the following lines. First, there are those who argue that it is an over-simplification which tends to ignore the many, varied, and complex cultural, social, and scientific factors involved. René Dubos points out that other civilizations, such as the Chinese, Greek, and Moslem, which were informed by other religious traditions, contributed their share to deforestation, erosion, and the destruction of nature in many other ways.[5]

Second, White's claim that the biblical creation myths express a view of the created order as existing simply for man's rule and benefit has been questioned by a number of biblical scholars and theologians.[6] White, they claim, mistakenly isolated the dominion formulation of Genesis 1:28 from the context of the entire chapter, which is concerned with a universal and divine hierarchy and a harmony in which human beings peacefully coexist with and are responsible for nature. The often-ignored verse 29, with its implied vegetarianism, certainly imposes stringent limits on human dominion. In this context, "to have dominion over" means to be a steward of the lower orders of creation. Furthermore, man's naming of the animals (Genesis 2:20) in the second story of creation does not mean, as White claims, the establishment of man's dominion over them. Since for the early Hebrews a name contained the essence of that which is named, the point of man's naming the animals in this story is simply that the animals now have a distinct and real existence in the totality of the created order. Again, while man occupies the highest level in the world's hierarchical order created by God, this status entails neither an arrogance toward nature nor a triumphant subjugation of it, for stress is placed on man's oneness with the earth (v. 7) and his responsibility for its keeping (v. 15). In chapter 3 of Genesis the further point is made that the fate of the created world depends on man's situation before God. In terms of their entire contexts, then, the perspective presented in biblical creation myths is a dialectical tension between humanity's transcendence of and radical oneness with the rest of creation.

Third, while White's proposal that ecologists select Saint Francis as a patron saint may be appropriate, his claim that Saint Francis advocated a radically alternative view of nature and man's relation to it which entailed the *spiritual autonomy* of *all parts of nature* and the *equality* of all creatures[7] is questionable. Indeed, it seems to be the case that Saint Francis viewed reality, heavenly and terrestrial, in terms of hierarchical gradations. The celestial hierarchy (God the Father, the Virgin Mary, God's beloved Son, and the Holy Spirit) are rulers of the universe, in relation to whom all created life is graded in orderly submission. All of the ordered gradations of the universe are created and preserved by the divine love.[8] In the famous *Canticle of Brother Sun*, Saint Francis insists at the very beginning that it is God alone who is to be praised, and according to some contemporary scholars, the correct rendering is not that God is praised by the creatures mentioned, but that he is to be praised *through* or *on account of* them. This view appears to find support in the *Mirror of Perfection*, in which it is said that the *Canticle* was written about "the things the Lord has created, *which we use every day*, without which we cannot live, yet with which humanity gives great offence to its Creator [by abusing them.]"[9] Although Saint Francis embraced and recommended poverty and humility, he himself engaged in work and included work as one of the imperatives for the friars in the Rules of 1221 and 1223. Those friars who had a trade were to work at it, and they were allowed to have the *tools* which they needed for their trade.[10] Surely this implies man's mastery over at least certain aspects of nature. It seems to be the case, then, that the dialectical tension between human transcendence of and radical oneness with nature expressed in the biblical view was also present in Saint Francis's perspective. Even though in his manner of life he may have placed greater emphasis on the pole of radical oneness with nature, the other pole of human transcendence of nature was not lacking from his perspective.

Fourth, in a response to his critics,[11] White affirms that while contemporary biblical exegesis may yield results which support respect for nature, this was not the case in the exegesis of earlier times in Western Christendom. Rather, he claims, it is "a fact that historically Latin Christians have generally been arrogant toward nature."[12] At the very least, this is a very sweeping generalization, one which is difficult to refute because of White's use of the vague qualifying term "generally," for any counterexamples may be discounted with the claim that they do not fall under the rubric of "generally." Furthermore, White seems to assume that instances of an effective use of nature by human beings necessarily implies that they are arrogant toward it. Even if it could be shown that *some* Latin Christians were arrogant toward nature, it would be wrong to make this charge against two of the most important and influential Latin Fathers, namely, Saint Augustine and Saint Thomas Aquinas. Since both held to creation *ex nihilo,* both affirmed that all natural things are ordained by the supreme art of the Creator, imitate the divine goodness, and are essentially good.[13] Augustine used the metaphor of a book, claiming that created things constitute God's great book written without ink.[14] Surely, this perspective is just the opposite of an arrogant attitude toward nature. Although nature is viewed neither as divine nor as an object of worship, it does have a derived dignity as the handiwork or art of God. Of course, like Saint Francis, Augustine and Aquinas viewed all reality as hierarchically structured in ordered gradations, with man occupying the highest rank in the created order. Augustine affirmed that man as a rational creature is more excellent than all the other creatures of the earth, but at the same time he declared that "even the most diminutive insect cannot be considered attentively without astonishment and without praising the Creator."[15] He also referred to what man has in common with the inanimate and animate creatures which occupy the lower ranks in the created order.[16] Aquinas affirmed that less noble creatures exist for the nobler, but in the same context he declared: "Every creature exists for its own proper act and perfection. . . . Furthermore, each and every creature exists for the perfection of the entire universe. Further still, the entire universe, with all its parts, is ordained towards God as its end, inasmuch as it imitates, as it were, and shows forth the divine goodness to the glory of God."[17] In light of even this brief sketch, it appears that the Augustinian-Thomistic view of man's relation to nature reflects the biblical perspective, namely, that there is a dialectical tension between humanity's transcendence of and radical oneness with the rest of creation.

It would seem to be the case that this dialectical and dipolar view asserts an obvious truth, confirmed by common human experience, and thus is more realistic than either a spiritualistic idealism which tends to ignore humanity's oneness with nature or a deistic romanticism which tends to ignore humanity's transcendence of nature. It is this latter view which appears to be the presupposition of White's position. In a rather ambiguous statement White claims that "we must rethink and refeel our nature and destiny."[18] In one sense this is impossible, since our nature is a given and our destiny has not yet arrived. Obviously White means that we do not properly or truly understand who or what we are and what purpose there might be in our existence. We need to reconsider our understanding so as to arrive at a position in which we discard, or at least minimize, the pole of human transcendence of nature in favor of emphasizing the spiritual autonomy of all aspects of nature and human oneness with all creatures. Those who support a theology of Christian "realism" with its dialectical and dipolar perspective concerning man's relation to nature find this view inadequate, and might well claim that it is mistaken because it elevates a half-truth to the position of a whole truth. It is an obvious fact that even though all creatures may have rights, they are not all *equal*, that human beings to some degree do in fact transcend nature. Among those who have held to a dialectical perspective was the American theologian, Reinhold Niebuhr. His dialectical and biblically oriented theology has often been called a theology of Christian realism. While his writings contain little with respect to an explicit consideration of environmental issues, it may prove interesting and instructive to consider briefly the implications of his thought for these issues.

Niebuhr's approach to Christian apologetics was polemical, dialectical, and open-ended in terms of both method and content. He attacked those views which would force a simple coherence upon experience and thus ignore or distort some of the facts of human life in order to establish their doctrines.[19] Among those views which are subject to this failure, Niebuhr believed, are the alternative positions of idealism and naturalism or rationalism and romanticism. Each tends to exaggerate the facts which support its own doctrine and to ignore those which support the alternative doctrine. The biblical understanding is superior to any one of these alternative doctrines precisely because it is not blind to the paradoxical character of the human condition. Of course, such a perspective cannot be contained within the confines of a tidy, coherent metaphysical system. Yet it is not irrational, Niebuhr claimed, for it is truer to the facts of human experience than either alternative analysis.[20]

Given his dialectical method, it is not surprising that Niebuhr's theology was dialectical in content. Nowhere is this more obvious than in his doctrine of man, in which he emphasized the dialectical tension between man's transcendence of nature and his oneness with it. Man, Niebuhr claimed, is that creature who stands at the juncture of nature and spirit. Like other creatures he is subject to the laws and limitations of nature, but unlike other creatures he can transcend both nature and himself through his consciousness and freedom. In the first volume of *The Nature and Destiny of Man* Niebuhr expressed this theme rather vividly when he said:

> The obvious fact is that man is a child of nature, subject to its vicissitudes, compelled by its necessities, driven by its impulses, and confined within the brevity of the years which nature permits its varied organic forms, allowing them some, but not too much, latitude. The other less obvious fact is that man is a spirit who stands outside of nature, life, himself, his reason and the world. . . . Man cannot, by taking thought, reduce himself to the proportions of nature and . . . he does not have the freedom to destroy his freedom over natural process, any more than he has the freedom to overcome his precarious dependence upon nature.[21]

Thus, man is both a "creature of necessity and the child of freedom."[22] He is never merely an element in nature, for his life is not wholly determined but is partially, at least, self-determining. It is this capacity for transcendence, for freedom, which is the basis for the uniqueness of the human self and distinguishes man from the other creatures.[23] It enables him to extend an impulse of nature beyond the limits it has in nature, to use the forces and processes of nature creatively. Yet it is precisely because of this freedom of spirit that man, unlike other creatures, can deny the limits of his finite existence and defy the forms and restraints of both nature and reason.

Since he is suspended between finitude and freedom, man

experiences a deep-seated anxiety or insecurity which, although not itself sin, is the precondition of sin. That is, man seeks to escape the discomfort of anxiety by abolishing either one or the other of the dual aspects of his nature. If he seeks to abolish his freedom, his self-transcendence, he falls into sensuality. If he seeks to abolish his finitude, to evade nature, he falls into pride. Niebuhr placed greater emphasis on pride because he viewed it as more basic than sensuality and because in part the latter is derived from the former. Like Augustine he views sin as being a matter of the will rather than of the flesh, and claimed that its most insidious form is pride. While pride has many faces, it manifests itself primarily in pride of power, pride of knowledge, and pride of virtue. It is at the higher and more established levels of human life, Niebuhr insists, that the pretension of self, the sin of pride, is most dangerous, precisely because it is a mixture of self-sufficiency and insecurity. Thus, he said: "The more man establishes himself in power and glory, the greater is the fear of tumbling from his eminence, or losing his treasure, or being discovered in his pretension. . . . Man seeks to make himself God because he is betrayed by both his greatness and his weakness; and there is no level of greatness and power in which the lash of fear is not at least one strand in the whip of ambition."[24]

Given his view of divine creation, of the image of God in man, Niebuhr claimed that sin, the pretension of self, is not an ontological necessity, a defect of essential human nature. It is a *corruption* of man's true essence, of what God has created in him, rather than its *destruction*. Thus man knows that he ought to act so as to contribute to the harmony of the whole, but his actual actions are always infected with the ambition to make himself the center of the whole. All human beings do in fact sin, and this results in estrangement not only in man's relation to God, others, and himself, but also in his relation to nature. In his sin man disturbs the tranquilities and harmonies of nature, throwing them out of joint. He transforms nature's harmless will-to-live into a sinful will-to-power.[25] Thus, in terms of a Christian realism like Niebuhr's, the root cause of our ecological crisis is man's sin. If faulty understanding is a part of the causal conditions, that too is due to sin which inclines man to rationalization in the attempt to justify his prideful egoism.

Niebuhr not only emphasized the dialectical tension in the human self and in the human relation to nature, but also acknowledged the obvious dialectical tension between order and disorder, harmony and disharmony, in nature itself. In an attack on the view that the source of sin lies in man's kinship with the lower creatures, in his animal nature corrupting his spirit, Niebuhr proclaimed: "To explain human evil in these terms is to forget that there is no sin in nature. Animals live in the harmony assigned to them by nature. If this harmony is not perfect and sets species against species in the law of the jungle, no animal ever aggravates, by his own decision, the disharmonies which are, with restricted harmonies, the condition of its life."[26] Since morality is a human capacity made possible by freedom, only human beings transform nature's harmless will-to-live into a sinful will-to-power. On one point, at least, Niebuhr agreed with Hume, namely, that the forces of nature are morally indifferent.[27] Even to the extent that "nature reveals a pre-established harmony, it is not moral but amoral."[28] It follows, then, that nature is not to be romanticized or worshiped. Yet, given the doctrine of creation,[29] the derived worth of nature is to be affirmed.

Another realm to which Niebuhr applied his dialectical perspective was that of science and technology. Given their capacity for freedom and transcendence, human beings not only have indeterminate possibilities for good but also indeterminate possibilities for evil. The extensions of human power over nature increase those possibilities for good and evil. In itself power, like nature, is not evil but amoral. Nevertheless, just as justice may be put into the service of love, so power may be put into the service of justice, of the attaining of the relatively good ends of justice.[30] But given faulty human imagination compounded with human egoism, there is always the abuse of power, the use of it in the service of unjust and evil ends. This is precisely the case with respect to the extension of man's power over nature in science and technology.

Long before there was much awareness of the dangers arising from technology and in a time when, so to speak, the laboratory was a sanctuary, the scientist a high priest, and the technologist an acolyte, Niebuhr warned that modern man's confidence in science and technology as the messiahs of a utopian age was naïve and mistaken. This confidence was misplaced he said, because it failed to take into account the fact that power and freedom contain destructive, as well as creative, possibilities.[31] To be sure, the achievements of modern knowledge and science were to be preferred to ignorance and obscurantism.[32] Many technical advances, such as those which freed men from grinding toil, held out the promise of emancipation from poverty, and eliminated age-old diseases, do indeed have beneficial effects.[33] Yet "science can sharpen the fangs of ferocity as much as it can alleviate human pain," for "intelligence merely raises all the potencies of life, both good and evil."[34]

Man's extension of his power over nature through science and technology tempts him to ignore his creatureliness in the pride of knowledge and power and to seek to elevate himself to the status of ultimacy. Such an attempt "offends not only against God, who is the centre and source of existence, but against other life which has a rightful place in the harmony of the whole."[35] The power of men, "by which they intend to protect themselves against other life, tempts them to destroy and oppress other life."[36] But sooner or later there is an inevitable reaction, and the destroyers become the destroyed. The same technical advances which created the possibility of a global community in which human beings could be freed to a large extent from the old evils of poverty and disease also increased the destructive power of the weapons of warfare so that all life on this globe stands under the threat of annihilation. The culprit in this situation, however, is not technology, but man's use of it. It is absurd to lament the existence of technological skills or to advocate "turning the clock back" to a pretechnological age. The viable issue today concerns the control and use of technology such that it can be made to enhance both the environment and human life instead of destroying them. For Niebuhr, the inspiration for and ultimate norm of acting in the world for the harmony of the whole and the good of all creatures is the self-giving love or *agape* of God as disclosed in Jesus Christ. This is the one absolute which, even though it transcends history, is relevant to history as the criterion in light of which ever greater degrees of justice, equity, and harmony should be sought for in actual concrete situations. That is, Niebuhr's Christian ethics is a contextualism in which attention is given to the actualities of the concrete situation, the *agape* absolute, and the middle principles and proximate goals of justice, equity, and harmony.

A fifth realm to which Niebuhr applied his dialectical perspective was that of the relation of individual to community. It is precisely because of human freedom, he believed, that this relation is unique and dialectical. Given the social character of man's existence and the fact that the human self is involved in an intricate relation of self-seeking and self-giving, the dialectical relation of individual to community is inevitable.[37] With respect to the political community, for example, it is man's capacity for self-giving and for justice which makes democracy possible, but, on the other hand, it is his inclination for self-seeking and injustice which makes democracy necessary.[38] Paradoxically, it is in those very relationships that require self-giving, namely, man's communities, that the egoisms of individuals become compounded such that the collective self-regard of the several human communities—social, economic, political, national, and religious—is more stubborn and persistent than the egoism of individuals. Niebuhr made this point in an early book which he entitled *Moral Man and Immoral Society*.[39] Later he affirmed that a better title would have been *The Not So Moral Man in His Less Moral Communities*.[40] Whatever the appropriate title, the argument was that groups or communities in the defense of perceived vested interests tend to violate the moral principles which are regarded as obligatory for individuals and at the same time to proclaim that they are the virtuous defenders of the faith, of democracy, or of some other noble cause. Every nation, for example, regards itself as more virtuous than its allies or enemies, no matter how immoral its actions may be.

Given this self-righteousness of collective egoisms, there are no simple or easy solutions for the social evils which plague mankind. Thus, the Niebuhrian position is diametrically opposed to what may be called the naïve "dominoes" views of both conservative evangelicals and secular and religious liberals. The former think that the "saving of souls" will automatically result in the solving of social problems, while the latter hope "to change the social situation by beguiling the egoism of individuals, either by adequate education or by pious benevolence."[41] It is this latter view which seems to be presupposed in the position of Lynn White. In terms of the argument in his article he appears to think that the solution of our environmental crisis lies in reeducating persons so that in thought and feeling they become aware of the equality of creatures in nature and the spiritual autonomy of all parts of nature. In light of Niebuhr's dialectical theology of Christian realism, this is inad-

equate for two reasons. First, it fails to recognize the sub-
tlety and power of individual sinful egoism, and second, it
ignores the stubbornness and persistence of collective egoism. Our present environmental crisis is due not only to the
wrongheaded thinking and mistaken feelings present in individuals because of their sinful egoism but also to the perceived vested interests, the collective egoism, of groups, social, economic, political, and religious. For example, in his
better moments an individual executive of an industry
might be persuaded of the need to be concerned about the
environment, and yet, because of his own ego interests and
the vested interest of the firm, he might be unable to restrain this industry from polluting the environment. Therefore, an effective amelioration of the present situation requires a multifarious strategy which includes attempts to
change both individuals and groups.

Given his view that past and contemporary history dem-
onstrates both the moral and the predatory, the self-giving
and the self-seeking, in all human activity, and especially in
man's collective activity, it is not surprising that Niebuhr
insisted that an effective strategy for social action involves
the dialectic of persuasion and coercion. He expressed this
rather vividly when he said:

> Sentimental moralism which underestimates the necessity of
> coercion, and cynical realism which is oblivious to the pos-
> sibilities of moral suasion are equally dangerous to the welfare
> of mankind. The former spends its energies in vain efforts to
> achieve a purely voluntary reorganization of society; the latter
> resorts to violent conflict and makes confusion worse con-
> founded. The welfare of society demands that enough social
> intelligence and moral idealism be created to prevent social
> antagonism from issuing in pure conflict and that enough so-
> cial pressure be applied to force reluctant beneficiaries of social
> privilege to yield their privileges before injustice prompts to
> vehemence and violence.[42]

Obviously, Niebuhr's concern in this statement was directed toward the end of achieving the equity and justice for the various races and classes that is necessary for the welfare of society. Yet the recommended strategy of persuasion and coercion has a wider application. It is an effective strategy for dealing with our environmental crisis, for producing those changes in society that are required for the control and redirection of technology so that the environment will be protected and enhanced. Yet the practical ways in which this strategy is employed must be evaluated in light of the *agape* norm and the middle principles.

In terms of Niebuhr's theology of Christian realism, however, not even those who engage in moral crusades, who use persuasion and coercion for noble ends, are exempt from the temptation to self-righteousness. Indeed, they are especially vulnerable to this temptation, for it is all too easy for those who work for noble ends to fall prey to the delusion that by so doing they have been transformed into sinless saints. But the fact of the matter is that they, too, remain sinners, subject to prideful egoism. Thus, in Niebuhr's view, all who work for noble ends should do so with humility and uneasy consciences. Of course, this applies also to those of us who support environmental reforms. For example, like the supporters of other causes, we are sometimes subject to the moral myopia of assuming that environmentalism is the only issue of prime importance in today's world, and thus we tend to ignore the cries of the dispossessed, the poor, and the distressed in our society and elsewhere. We, too, often need to confess, in the words of the Book of Common Prayer, "We have left undone those things which we ought to have done." While the care and healing of the environment is an imperative and indeed a divine imperative, there are other imperatives which should not be ignored. There are many other ways in which our prideful egoism raises barriers to the actualization of the very objectives to which we are committed. The recognition that we are not sinless saints, that our actions on behalf of noble causes need to be accompanied by uneasy consciences and humility, is, in Niebuhr's view, a necessary condition for genuinely effective social action. Obviously it follows that it is a *sine qua non* for actualizing those changes in society required for the sake of the environment.

In light of this brief analysis, my conclusion is that in Reinhold Niebuhr's theology is to be found a better undergirding for environmental ethics and a more effective strategy for action than in the theology presupposed in positions similar to that of Lynn White, Jr. While Niebuhr's Christocentric theology, his theology of revelation, may need to be supplemented with a natural theology like that found in process theology, it is preferable to that presupposed by White even without such a supplement. Niebuhr's dialectical and dipolar approach seeks to describe man and nature as they are rather than in a romanticist or idealistic manner. This realism, however, does not sink to the level of pessimism. The amelioration of evil situations is possible even though no utopia will ever be achieved in human history. Such amelioration is possible because man possesses indeterminate possibilities for good as well as for evil. In the Niebuhrian view, then, the Christian and the Christian church, conscious of the *agape* norm, should seek to understand and act in concrete situations in terms of the middle principles of justice, equity, and harmony for the purpose of actualizing the closest approximation of *agape* possible in those concrete situations. With respect to the current environmental crisis this obviously means that the Christian and the church should be concerned with contributing in whatever ways are possible to the task of protecting and enhancing the environment, of making this earth clean, sweet, and habitable for all creatures now living as well as for the as yet unborn generations.

Notes

1. Cited by Gabriel Fackre, "Ecology and Theology," in *Western Man and Environmental Ethics*, ed. Ian G. Barbour (Reading, Mass.: Addison-Wesley, 1973), p. 117.
2. This article appeared originally in *Science* 155 (1967): 1203–7. It is to be found also in several anthologies, such as Barbour, ed., *Western Man and Environmental Ethics*, pp. 18–30; Garret De Bell, ed., *The Environmental Handbook* (New York: Ballantine Books, 1970); Jacob Needleman et al., eds., *Religion for a New Generation*, 2d ed. (New York: Macmillan, 1977), pp. 231–39. This last work is the source of my quotations from White's article.
3. Ibid., p. 239.
4. Ibid., p. 238.
5. "A Theology of the Earth," in *Western Man and Environmental Ethics*, ed. Barbour, p. 46.
6. See Fackre, "Ecology and Theology," pp. 116–24; *The Interpreter's Dictionary of the Bible*, supp. vol. (Nashville: Abingdon Press, 1976), pp. 247–48.
7. White, "Historical Roots," p. 239.
8. See Ray C. Petry, ed., *Late Medieval Mysticism*, Library of Christian Classics, vol. 13 (Philadelphia: Westminster Press, 1957), pp. 116–19.
9. Cited by John Holland Smith, *Francis of Assisi* (London: Sidgwick and Jackson, 1972), p. 1974. Italics are mine.
10. See Benen Fahy and Placid Hermann, *The Writings of St. Francis of Assisi* (Chicago: Franciscan Herald Press, 1963), pp. 37–38, 61, 68.
11. Barbour, ed., *Western Man and Environmental Ethics*, pp. 55–64.
12. Ibid., p. 61.
13. See Augustine, *City of God*, 12.4; Aquinas, *Summa Theologica*, 1–2, q. 13, art. 3; *Summa Contra Gentiles*, 3.20.
14. *Sermon*, Mai (126:6; cited in *The Essential Augustine*, ed. Vernon J. Bourke (Indianapolis: Hacket, 1964), p. 123.
15. *City of God*, 22.24.
16. Ibid., 5.11.

17. *Summa Theologica*, 1, q. 65, art. 2.

18. Needleman, *Religion for a New Generation*, p. 239.

19. See Reinhold Niebuhr, "Coherence, Incoherence and Christian Faith," *Christian Realism and Political Problems* (New York: Charles Scribner's Sons, 1953), pp. 175–203; "As Deceivers, Yet True," in *Beyond Tragedy* (New York: Charles Scribner's Sons, 1937), pp. 3–24.

20. See Reinhold Niebuhr, *The Nature and Destiny of Man*, vol. 1 (New York: Charles Scribner's Sons, 1943), especially chaps. 1–3, pp. 1–92.

21. Ibid., pp. 3, 99.

22. Niebuhr, *Beyond Tragedy*, p. 292–93.

23. See Reinhold Niebuhr, *The Self and the Dramas of History* (New York: Charles Scribner's Sons, 1955), pp. 3–5.

24. Niebuhr, *The Nature and Destiny of Man*, vol. 1, pp. 193–94.

25. Ibid., p. 41; Niebuhr, *Beyond Tragedy*, pp. 11, 103, 266.

26. Niebuhr, *Beyond Tragedy*, p. 294.

27. Ibid., p. 97.

28. Ibid., p. 241.

29. See Niebuhr, *The Nature and Destiny of Man*, 1:131–36; Niebuhr, *Faith and History* (New York: Charles Scribner's Sons, 1949), pp. 46–50.

30. See Reinhold Niebuhr, *Love and Justice*, ed. D. B. Robertson (Philadelphia: Westminster Press, 1957), p. 300.

31. See Niebuhr, *Faith and History*, pp. 87, 100.

32. Niebuhr, *Beyond Tragedy*, p. 125.

33. Ibid., p. 99.

34. Ibid., pp. 125–26.

35. Ibid., p. 102.

36. Ibid., p. 103.

37. See Reinhold Niebuhr, *Man's Nature and His Communities* (New York: Charles Scribner's Sons, 1965), pp. 106–7.

38. See Reinhold Niebuhr, *The Children of Light and the Children of Darkness* (New York: Charles Scribner's Sons, 1944), p. xi.

39. Reinhold Niebuhr, *Moral Man and Immoral Society* (New York: Charles Scribner's Sons, 1932).

40. Niebuhr, *Man's Nature and His Communities*, p. 22.

41. Ibid.
42. Reinhold Niebuhr, "Moralists and Politics," in *Essays in Applied Christianity*, ed. D. B. Robertson, (New York: Meridian Books, 1959), pp. 80–81. This article first appeared in the *Christian Century*, 6 July 1932.

John B. Cobb, Jr.

Christian Existence in a World of Limits

A world which once seemed open to almost infinite expansion of human population and economic activity now appears as a world of limits. Christians are hardly more prepared for life and thought in this world than are any other groups, despite the fact that Christian understanding and ethics were shaped in a world of limits. Those of us who are Christian need to recover aspects of our heritage that are relevant to our current situation and to offer them for consideration in the wider domain as well. Accordingly, this essay first describes the recognition of limits as these now appear to many sensitive people and then reviews features of the Christian tradition that may today inform appropriate responses.

The finitude of our planet requires us to work toward a human society that accepts limits and seeks a decent life for all within them. Such a society should live in balance with other species and primarily on the renewable resources of the planet. It should use nonrenewable resources only at a rate that is agreed upon in light of technological progress in safe substitution of more plentiful resources. The emission of waste into the environment should be within the capacity of that environment to purify itself. By shifting primarily to solar energy, thermal pollution would be kept to a minimum.

Whereas the goal of universal affluence has led to increasing economic interdependence of larger and larger regions, until we have become a global economic unity, the goal of living within renewable resources lies in the opposite direction. Relative economic independence of smaller regions is preferable. Whereas the goal of universal affluence has directed industry and agriculture to substitute energy and materials for human labor, the new goal will severely qualify this. Labor-saving devices are certainly not to be despised, but much production will need to be more labor-intensive than is that of the overdeveloped world today. Whereas the goal of universal affluence has led us to encourage the application of scientific knowledge about chemistry and physics to technology and production, restricting this only when the dangers could be demonstrated beyond reasonable doubt, the goal of living within renewable resources will put the burden of proof on the other side. A new product will be allowed only when it is shown beyond reasonable doubt not to damage the long-term capacity of the planet to support life. Whereas we have pursued universal affluence chiefly by increasing the total quantity of goods and services available, and we have concerned ourselves only secondarily about their distribution, the goal of living within renewable resources forces a reversal. Since global growth will be limited, and since in many areas there must be substantial reduction of production, appropriate distribution of goods to all becomes the primary concern.

Clearly these shifts are drastic. Our present economic system is geared to the goal of affluence and is quite inappropriate to the new goal. Our political system is intimately bound up with our economic system. Our agriculture has now been largely absorbed by our industrial capitalism. Our cities are designed so as to require maximum amounts of consumption and hence of production. Our international policies are geared to support this way of life.

Merely to sketch some ingredients of the order which is needed is to become aware of limits at another point. We have limited ability even to conceive a way of moving to the kind of society we need or to enter seriously into willing the steps that would be required. We are like passengers on a train whose brakes have failed and which is rushing down a slope toward a broken bridge. We point to a spot above us on the mountainside, reached by no tracks, and say that should be our destination.

Further, even these changes would not work without stability of global population, and the limits beyond which a decent life for all is impossible will almost certainly have been reached in some parts of the globe before voluntary control will effect such stability. In addition, even if adverse effects on planetary climate by human activity are greatly curtailed, the favorable weather of these past decades is not likely to last, and we must reckon with the probability that it will be difficult to continue to increase food production. Hence, implementation of the policies indicated, while curtailing catastrophe, would not prevent large-scale suffering. The recognition of limits must include the recognition that we cannot prevent the occurrence of manifold types of evil.

The notion that human capacity to overcome poverty or even to prevent starvation is limited comes to us as a shock. This shock shows how deeply we have been shaped by our recent history. It presupposes that we view ourselves as the creators of history, able to fashion it according to our rational purposes. Such an idea was unknown before the late eighteenth century. Already in the mid-nineteenth century it was subject to ridicule by leading humanists and philosophers who saw in supposed human progress the death of Western civilization. Nevertheless, the continuing increase in the capacity of human beings to exploit and alter the environment, the advance of science, the extension of creature comforts, and the "conquest" of space have reinforced the sense of human omnipotence that came to expression in the idea of progress. We Americans, especially, feel that we *should* be able to prevent the deterioration of the world.

The assumption of responsibility for the world, even in its nineteenth-century expressions, was bound up with a sense that there is a force for progress that is deeper than our individual choices. Marx found a dialectical process at work in the economic order. Comte envisaged an evolution from the theological to the metaphysical stages of history, which is now realizing the positive stage. People are called to join in a struggle where the winning cards are already on their side. In this view, history is now triumphing over its age-old limits.

If instead we see that the dominant forces of history are rushing toward catastrophe, we confront the question of limits in a new way. Even if we can conceive forms of society that would make possible a just and attractive life in a physically limited world, are we human beings capable of personal changes of the magnitude required for the constitution of such societies? The old debate about human nature takes on new importance. Are we naturally good, so that when distorting social pressures are removed we will enter into humane and appropriate patterns of life? Are we naturally competitive and acquisitive, so that only imposed social controls can maintain a measure of order? Are we neutrally capable of either good or evil, so that everything depends on our individual acts of will?

Only the first of these three theories offers hope for a successful adaptation to physical limits, and unfortunately the evidence does not support it. Our genetic endowment is shaped by earlier epochs in which those communities survived that nurtured affection and cooperation within, but enmity toward competing groups. Those communities whose males were averse to violence did not survive in the more desirable regions of the globe. Genetic tendencies have been accentuated in those cultures which have been most successful in history, so that deeply entrenched cultural conditioning reinforces personal attitudes and habits that resist needed changes. There is naturalistic reason to doubt that the human species has the requisite capacity to change.

There is danger today that those who understand our situation most profoundly will despair. Despair leads to inaction. Unless hope can live in the midst of openness to truth, our situation is indeed desperate. The Christian faith has been one important way in which people have lived with hope in the midst of conditions that appeared, objectively, hopeless. It is the way which I know as a participant, and it is to the exposition of this way that the remainder of this essay is devoted.

Christianity does not underestimate the strength of tendencies which in the course of history have become anti-human and now threaten our survival. Viewing our ordinary ways of feeling, thinking, and acting in the light of Jesus, Christians have used language like "natural depravity." But we also recognize in ourselves a transcendence over genetic endowment and cultural conditioning that makes us both responsible and, in principle, free to change. We recognize in ourselves also a profound resistance to change, so that our freedom is not a matter of simple choice between good and evil. Our self-centeredness distorts our use of our freedom. But we discover that there is a power at work in us that can transform even our distorted wills. This transformation is not subject to our control but comes as a gift. We call it grace, and we can place no limits on the extent to which grace can make us into new men and new women.

Apart from the transformative power of grace, there would be no grounds of hope. We would have to resign ourselves to the inevitable or seek release from an unendurable world in mystical transcendence. Because of grace, resignation and release are not acceptable choices for Christians. We know that we are not masters of history, but neither are we mere victims. We need to identify appropriate options recognizing (1) the physical limits of our context and (2) the limits of our own capacities to envision needed change or to adopt even those changes we can envision, but also (3) the openness of the future and the unlimited power of transformation that is the grace of God. I propose five images of appropriate Christian response. There is some tension among them, and none of us are called to enter equally into all of them. It is my hope that we can support one another in our varied Christian decisions.

Christian Realism

By Christian realism I mean to point to that style of action described so brilliantly by Reinhold Niebuhr.[1] Niebuhr knew that the quest for justice in human affairs would not be consummated by the achievement of a just society. Every attainment of relative justice produces a situation in which new forms of injustice arise. There is no assurance that any amount of effort will lead to a society that is better than our own, and, even if it does, there is no assurance that the improvement will last. But this is no reason to relax our efforts. The maintenance of relative justice requires constant struggle.

In this struggle moral exhortation is of only limited use. People in large numbers are motivated by self- or group interest. Relative justice is obtained only as the competing groups within society arrive at relatively equal strength. Thus organized labor now receives relative justice in this society because labor unions have power comparable to that of capital.

Christian realists do not appeal to the United States on idealistic grounds alone to supply food to a world food bank.

They form alliances with those groups that stand to gain financially by such an arrangement or see political advantages to be won. Furthermore, they realize how fragile will be any agreement on the part of this country that is not clearly in its self-interest, and they work accordingly to strengthen the political power of those countries most in need of American largesse. Perhaps other suppliers of raw materials can follow the model of the OPEC countries in banding together, so as to be able to bargain better for what they need.

Christian realists know that influencing government policy requires hard work and shrewdness. They employ the best lobbyists they can find and bring as much sophisticated understanding as possible to bear on issues while exerting pressure through influencing public opinion. They know that the problems we are dealing with will be with us for the foreseeable future, and hence they settle in for the long haul rather than rely on a quadrennial emphasis on hunger or a special plea for compassionate action.

Christian realists see that the church itself has its own independent capacity to deal with global issues and that there are other nongovernmental organizations with which it needs to work closely. Rightly directing the energies of these private institutions may be as important as directly influencing government policy. Often government policy will follow directions pioneered by other institutions.

The Eschatological Attitude

Although Christian realism is a more appropriate response for American Christians than either moral exhortation or revolution, it has limitations. Its maximum achievement will be ameliorative. Since it accepts the existing structures of power, and since these structures are part of the total world-system that moves toward catastrophe, Christian realism alone is not an adequate Christian response. Although any direct attempt to overthrow the existing system would be counterproductive, that system may well collapse of its own weight. It would be unfortunate if Christians became so immersed in a "realistic" involvement in existing institutions that they could not respond creatively to the opportunity that may be offered to build different ones.

Some Christians may elect to live now in terms of what they envision as quite new possibilities for human society even when they do not know how to get from here to there. We may not know how to bring about a society that uses only renewable resources, but we can experiment with life styles that foreshadow that kind of society. We may not know how to provide the Third World with space and freedom to work out its own destiny, but in the name of a new kind of world we can withdraw our support from the more obvious structures of oppression. We may not know how to shift from a growth-oriented economy to a stationary-state economy, but we can work out the principles involved in such an economy.

To exert energies in these ways is not to live in an irrelevant world of make-believe. It is to live from a hopeful future. It may not affect the course of immediate events as directly as will the policy of Christian realism, but it may provide the stance that will make it possible, in a time of crisis, to make constructive rather than destructive changes. Even if the hoped-for future never comes, the choice of living from it may not be wrong. The Kingdom expected by Jesus' disciples did not arrive, but the energies released by that expectation and the quality of lives of those who lived from that future deeply affected the course of events in unforeseen and unintended ways. To live without illusion in the spirit of Christian realism may turn out in the long run to be less "realistic" than to shape our lives from visions of a hopeful future.

To live eschatologically in this sense is not simply to enjoy hopeful images from time to time. The hope for the Kingdom freed early Christians from concern for success or security in the present order. Similarly, for us today to live from the future will mean quite concretely that we cease to try to succeed and to establish our security in the present socioeconomic order. For most of us that would be a radical change, and many would say it is "unrealistic." But unless there are those Christians who have inwardly disengaged themselves from our present structures, we will not be able to offer leadership at a time when there might be readiness for such leadership.

The Discernment of Christ

Most dedication to social change has involved the belief that history is on the side of the change. Christians have made the stronger claim that they were working to implement God's will. When God is understood as omnipotent, Christians have an assurance of ultimate success for their causes regardless of the more immediate outcome of the efforts. But today we do not perceive God as forcing divine decisions upon the world. Every indication is that the human species is free to plunge into catastrophes of unprecedented magnitude if it chooses to do so.

If we no longer think of God as on our side ensuring the success of our undertakings, we can and should seek all the more to discern where Christ as the incarnate Logos is at work in our world. When we look for Christ we do not seek displays of supernormal force but quiet works of creative love, or the still small voice. Bonhoeffer did well when he pointed away from a controlling deity and spoke of the divine suffering. But he was dangerously misleading when he spoke of the divine as powerless. The still small voice and the man on the cross have their power, too, but it is a different sort of power from that of the thunderbolt and the insurance company's "acts of God."

If our eyes are opened by faith, we see Christ wherever we look. We see him in the aspirations for justice and freedom on the part of the oppressed and in the glimmering desire of the oppressor to grant justice and freedom. He appears most strikingly in the miracle of conversion when something radically new enters a person's life and all that was there before takes on changed meaning. But we see him less fully formed in a child struggling to understand, or in a gesture of sympathy to an injured dog. Wherever a human being is reaching out from herself or himself, wherever there is growth toward spirit, wherever there is hunger for God, wherever through the interaction of people a new intimacy comes into being, we discern the work and presence of Christ. Equally, we experience Christ in challenges that threaten us and in opportunities we have refused. Christ appears also in the emergence of new ideas and insights, in the creativity of the artist, and in the life of the imagination, for Christ is that which makes all things new, and without newness there can be no thought, art, or imagination.

In a situation where habits, established institutions, social and economic structures are leading us to destruction, Christ is our one hope. In quietness and in unexpected places Christ is bringing something new to birth, something we cannot foresee and build our plans upon. As Christians we need to maintain an attitude of expectancy, open to accepting and following the new work of Christ. It may even be that Christ wants to effect some part of that important work in us, and we must be open to being transformed by it. We cannot produce that work, but we can attune ourselves and practice responsiveness to the new openings that come moment by moment.

The attitude I am now describing is different from Christian realism and Christian eschatology, but it is contradictory to neither. Ultimately, we should adopt the realist or eschatological stance only as we are led to do so by Christ, and we should remain in those postures only as we find Christ holding us there. That is to say, to live by faith is to live in readiness to subordinate our past plans and projects, even those undertaken in obedience to Christ, to the new word that is Christ today.

In the discernment of that word we need one another. It is easy to confuse Christ with our own desires or impulses or even our fears. Our ability to discriminate Christ is heightened by participation in a community which intends to serve him and which remembers the failures as well as the achievements of the past. But finally Christians know that they stand alone with Christ responding or failing to respond to the offer of new life through which they may also mediate Christ to others.

The Way of the Cross

Moltmann followed up his great book *The Theology of Hope* with another entitled *The Crucified God*.[2] He rightly recognized that, for the Christian, hope stands in closest proximity to sacrifice. Whereas in the sixties it was possible for some oppressed groups to believe that the forces of history were on their side and that they had suffered enough, the course of events has reminded us all that hope is not Christian if it is tied too closely to particular events and outcomes. We cannot circumvent the cross. Now as we face more clearly the limits of the human situation and the fact that poverty and suffering cannot be avoided even by the finest programs we could devise, we are forced to look again at the meaning of the cross for us. Have we affluent middle-class American Christians been avoiding the cross too long?

I am not suggesting that we should court persecution or that we adopt ascetic practices in order to suffer as others do. There is enough suffering in the world without our intentionally inflicting it upon ourselves. Whatever the future, we are called to celebrate all life, including our own, not to repress it. But the celebration of life does not involve participation in the luxury and waste of a throwaway society that exists in the midst of world poverty. More important, it does not mean that we float on down the stream because the current carries us effortlessly along. We are called to swim against the stream, at personal cost, and without expectation of understanding and appreciation. That is a serious and authentic way of bearing a cross.

Furthermore, in a world in which, globally, poverty is here to stay, we are called as Christians to identify with the poor. That has always been Christian teaching, but when we thought that our own affluence contributed to the spread of affluence around the world, we could evade that teaching. Now we know that riches can exist in one quarter only at the expense of the poverty of others. In a world divided between oppressor and oppressed, rich and poor, the Christian cannot remain identified with the oppressor and the rich.

The rhetoric of identification with the poor and the oppressed has been around for some time. We have to ask what it means, and here diversity is legitimate. For some it means functioning as advocates for the cause of the poor; for a few, joining revolutionary movements; for others, embracing poverty as a way of life. I believe this third meaning needs to be taken by Christians with increasing seriousness. The one who actually becomes poor will be a better advocate for the cause of the poor and freer to respond to other opportunities for identification.

I do not have in mind that we should dress in rags, go around with a begging bowl, or eat inferior food. That, too, may have its place, but I mean by poverty two things: first, and chiefly, disengagement from the system of acquiring and maintaining property and from all the values and involvements associated with it, and, secondly, frugality. The Catholic church has long institutionalized poverty of this sort. Protestants tried to inculcate frugality and generosity as a form of poverty to be lived in the world, but that experiment failed. Today we need to reconsider our earlier rejection of special orders so as to develop new institutions appropriate for our time. We can learn much from the Ecumenical Institute as well as from Taize.

I believe that the actual adoption of poverty as a way of life, supported by the churches, would strengthen the capacity of Christians to respond in all the ways noted above. The Christian realist is limited not only by the political powers with which he or she must deal but also by his or her own involvement in a way of life that the needed changes threaten. The Christian voice will speak with greater clarity and authenticity when it speaks from a life situation that is already adapted to the new condition that is needed. Although a life of poverty is not by itself a sufficient definition of living from the hoped-for future, it is an almost essential element in such a life. Our capacity to be sensitive to the call of Christ can be enhanced when we do not nurse a secret fear that he will speak to us as he did to the rich young ruler. Of course, there will be danger of self-righteousness and otherworldliness, but we have not escaped these dangers by abandoning special orders.

Prophetic Vision

"Where there is no vision, the people perish" (Proverbs 29:18). That proverb has a frighteningly literal application to our time. We simply will not move forward to the vast changes that are required without an attracting vision. But such vision is in short supply. There are still proposed visions of a future of increasing global affluence, but they are irrelevant to our present situation and encourage the wrong attitudes and expectations. There are images aplenty of catastrophe, but they breed a despair that is worse than useless. We need a prophetic vision of a world into which God might transform ours through transforming us.

This means that one particularly important response to our situation is openness to the transformation of our imagination. We live largely in and through our images. Where no adequate images exist, we cannot lead full and appropriate lives. In recent centuries church people have not been in the forefront of image making. We have increasingly lived in and from images fashioned by others. Our traditional Christian images have been crowded into special corners of our lives. Recognizing our poverty, we need to find Christ at work in other communities in the new creation of images by which we can be enlivened. We can hope also that as we confess our nakedness and gain a fresh appreciation for the creative imagination, the sickness of the church in this respect may be healed and our Christian faith can be released to share in the fashioning of the images so urgently needed.

Concretely we in this country need a prophetic vision of an economic order that is viable and humane with respect to our own people without continuing economic imperialism and environmental degradation. We need a vision of a global agriculture that can sustain the health of an increased population in the short run without worsening the opportunities of future generations or decimating other species of plants and animals. We need a vision of urban life that maximizes the social and cultural opportunities of cities while minimizing the destructive impact of our present cities both upon their inhabitants and upon the environment. We need a vision of personal existence in community that brings personal freedom into positive relation with mutual intimacy and individual difference into positive relation with mutual support. We need a vision of how the finest commitments of one generation can be transmitted to the next without oppression and so as to encourage free responsiveness to new situations.

We have bits and pieces of the needed vision. In my personal search I have found the most impressive breakthrough in the work of Paolo Soleri. But in all areas most of the work remains to be done. Vision in no sense replaces the need for rigorous reflection on details of both theory and practice. Instead, it gives a context in which hard work of mind and body takes on appropriate meaning.

Without vision the other types of response I have mentioned degenerate into legalism and self-righteousness. As the bearer of prophetic vision, the church could again become a center of vitality in a decaying world. But to bear prophetic vision is costly. It is not possible apart from some of the other responses noted above.

Conclusion

Perhaps the deepest level of our response to the awareness of limits is the recognition that we cannot free ourselves from guilt. We are caught in a destructive system, and we find that even our will to disidentify with that system is mixed with the desire to enjoy its fruits. None of us are innocent either in intention or behavior. At most we ask that we may be helped to open ourselves to re-creation by God, but we also depend on grace in another sense. It is only because we know ourselves accepted in our sinfulness that we can laugh at our own pretenses, live with a measure of joy in the midst of our halfheartedness, and risk transformation into a new creation.

Notes

1. Reinhold Niebuhr, *The Nature and Destiny of Man: A Christian Interpretation* (New York: Charles Scribner's Sons, 1941).
2. Jurgen Moltmann, *Theology of Hope: On the Ground and the Implication of a Christian Eschatology* (New York: Harper and Row, 1967), *The Crucified God* (New York: Harper and Row, 1974).

Jay McDaniel

Christianity and the Need for New Vision

W here there is no vision, the people perish" (Proverbs 29:18). This proverb can serve as a twofold reminder for Christianity today. It can be a reminder that the God of the biblical perspective is a friend rather than an enemy of the human imagination, especially as that imagination is directed toward the envisionment of new and hopeful futures. And it can be a reminder that there is urgent need today, within and outside Christianity, for new vision—that is, for vision conducive to the emergence of societies throughout the world that are peaceful, just, and ecologically sustainable.

My aim in this essay is to outline aspects of a new vision that can and should emerge within Christianity if Christians are to serve the needs of the global future. The new vision will be called an "ecological" perspective, and it will be compared and contrasted with a "substantialist" perspective that has informed much of the Christian past. As will be seen, the ecological perspective involves the view that the world is a complex network of interdependent forms of life, each with its own intrinsic value. By contrast, the substantialist perspective involves the idea that the world is a nexus of mutually external "substances" devoid of worth until assigned value by humans or by God. Whereas the substantialist mentality discourages an awareness of interconnectedness and diverse forms of value, the ecological perspective encourages that awareness. Such awareness is itself an essential precondition for styles of living that can yield peace, justice, and sustainability.

To speak of the ecological paradigm as *new*, of course, is not to suggest that it is without a heritage. On the contrary, ecological thinking has existed in numerous non-Western religious traditions, as well as in certain strands of Jewish and early Christian thought. Nevertheless, in relation to the dominant paradigm of post-biblical Christianity, the ecological paradigm *is* new. Post-biblical Christianity, as heavily influenced by Greek modes of thought, has been for the most part substantialist rather than ecological. God has been construed as a substance isolated from the world, the soul as a substance isolated from the body, humanity as a substance isolated from nature, and the church as a substance isolated from pagans. What is needed within Christianity is a vision that is new in comparison with this substantialist past.

Can Christianity open itself to possibilities for new vision? I suggest that it can. In the first section I discuss the way in which the current global situation and the prophetic heritage of the Bible require a contemporary openness to possibilities for new vision; in the second section I adumbrate the substantialist perspective as it has influenced certain features of the Christian past; and in the third section I discuss the ecological paradigm as it can influence the Christian future. Implicit in my discussion is the supposition that Christianity itself is an ongoing process capable of growth and change, rather than a settled and finished fact. This assumption is characteristic of the process or Whiteheadian theological perspective from which I proceed. As I suggest in the following section, the assumption is also characteristic of the prophetic strand of biblical thinking.

Jay McDaniel

The Need for Change Within Christianity

As a reading of the daily newspaper suggests, the global situation involves numerous problems that have, at face value, no simple solutions. The problems include poverty and hunger for over 50 percent of the world's human population, political repression for equal numbers, the ever-present threat of nuclear war, and the rampant and unchecked exploitation of natural systems on which human and other forms of life depend. The problem of ecological exploitation sometimes receives less attention than do the problems of poverty, repression, and war. Yet, the need to end such exploitation is crucial, both for the nonhuman realities that reap the consequences of abuse and for their human counterparts. As Lester Brown has shown, ecological destruction—as manifest in increasing rates of soil erosion, pollution, resource depletion, and biosystem destruction—is itself a cause of social tensions that induce poverty, repression, and war.[1] The holocaust that ends all wars may well result from economic tensions caused by international competition for diminishing resources or from food crises stemming from unchecked soil erosion in industrial and developing countries. Without new and ecologically responsible vision, the people, and much nonhuman life as well, may perish.

One area in which new vision is needed is that of social policy and social system. Nation-states and local communities must imagine modes of social organization that yield peace, justice, and environmental responsibility. Fortunately, significant vision is emerging among a creative minority of social thinkers. Examples include the thought of Amory and Hunter Lovins on soft energy paths, Herman Daly on steady-state economics, John Todd on alternative forms of community design, and the late E. F. Schumacher on appropriate technologies. Just as important, alternative communities are being established in which these theoretical visions can be tested and implemented. While such communities and the visions by which they are guided are largely unnoticed by those who currently set the domestic and foreign policies of nation-states, the significance of these alternatives should not be underestimated. As Robert C. Johansen has observed: "In a world where system change is desirable and necessary but where dominant institutions resist change, an extraordinary responsibility falls upon the individual citizen, religious communities, and other non-governmental agencies to bring about required changes."[2] Those who create alternative social visions and those who attempt to implement them may well provide the models toward which even nation-states must turn in the face of impending crises.

A second area in which new vision is needed is that of myth. By myth I mean the world view or imagistic lens through which a people conceive and perceive the data of experience. The three-tiered universe presupposed by ancient biblical authors is a world view of this sort, as is the mechanistic universe presupposed by modern science. While the former is predominantly imagistic and the latter predominantly conceptual, the difference is one of degree rather than kind. Both are myths or world views in terms of which individuals and societies interpret the world.

Myths and world views are important, not only because they guide humans in thought, feeling, and perception, but also because they guide them in action. Human beings respond to the data of experience in terms of mythic visions to which they consciously or unconsciously adhere. This means that social crises can be provoked by prevailing myths as well as by political and economic forces. Consider, for example, the myth of cosmic dualism cultivated for centuries by various civilizations. It involves the idea that "man" and "nature" are ontologically separable realities and that "nature" is primarily a tool for "man's" use. As feminist thinkers have rightly shown, this world view has spurred at least two forms of oppression: that of nature and that of women. Under the banner of dualism, nature has been approached almost exclusively as if it were an external power to be transformed by "man" into equipment for human use. And inasmuch as women have been symbolically identified with nature, they, too, have been approached by men as if they were external powers to be tamed and exploited. It is no accident that women and nature often have been raped, both literally and symbolically, by those who are guided by the myth of dualism.

Whether destructive or constructive, however, mythic world views are inescapable. When we criticize a given myth, we always do so from the point of view of another myth to which we subscribe. This means that movements of liberation, which criticize old myths, are themselves motivated by new myths. In much feminist literature, for example, a new myth is espoused in which humankind and non-human nature are pictured as two aspects of a single whole and in which nonhuman nature is said to have intrinsic as well as instrumental value. This new myth is an example of the ecological vision that will be discussed subsequently. The point here, however, is that it, too, is a myth. Myths are part of the very stuff of which human life consists.

At this point religion becomes especially relevant, for one of the functions of religion is to nurture myths by which people can live. Joining religion in this function are art and philosophy, and in recent times science. Historically, the record of accomplishment in religion is mixed. The religions of the world have produced myths by which people have lived, and they have produced myths by which people have been deprived of life. In this regard Christianity is no exception. The mythical past of the Christian heritage has been the source of laudable ideals concerning peace, social justice, love, and forgiveness. And yet, as evidenced in attitudes toward "heretics," non-Christians, and the natural world, the Christian heritage has also been the source of appalling ideals to the contrary. Under the auspices of a Christian world view, many have happily lived, but many others have unhappily died.

Is the future of Christianity defined by, and limited to, the totality of its mythical past? For the sake of a sane global future, let us hope not. Three examples will suffice. First, in light of impending ecological crises and the ongoing oppression of women, the world cannot survive a prolongation of dualistic attitudes concerning "man" and "nature." Yet such attitudes have been an integral part of what Christianity has espoused in the past. Second, in light of the ever-present threat of nuclear war, the world cannot survive a prolongation of attitudes in which the divine is envisioned as a holy warrior, bent upon destroying "his" enemies. Yet, such attitudes, too, have been an essential ingredient of the Christian past. And, third, in light of existing sociopolitical oppression, the world cannot survive attitudes that emphasize heavenly rewards over earthly needs. Yet, such attitudes, too, have been part of the Christian mythical heritage. In these respects and others, the preferred world of the future and the Christianity of the past cannot coexist.

At first, of course, a recognition of the deficiencies of the past comes as a shock to most Christians. Christians have a tendency to respond to a call for change defensively, as do other human beings. But Christianity itself stems from a biblical heritage in which change is often invited rather than feared. This is the prophetic and eschatological heritage of the Jewish Bible and the New Testament. The prophets of the Jewish Bible were fundamentally eschatological in their orientation. They experienced God, not as one who calls for a return to a primordial past, but rather as one who calls toward new and hopeful futures. In the words of Walter Brueggemann, the prophetic task was "to keep alive the

ministry of the imagination, to keep on conjuring alternative futures to the single one the king wants to urge as the
only thinkable one."³ And Jesus, the pivotal figure in Christian understanding, stands within the processive orientation
of this prophetic heritage. His imaginative anticipation of a
"kingdom of God"—a community of love and justice—ex-
emplifies the very hope for a new future that informed his
prophetic forebears. For Jesus, as for those that preceded
him, God seems to have been experienced as the ground of
hope: one who calls beyond what has been, toward what can
be.

If we analyze the attitude toward the past that this prophetic heritage embodies, we see that it involves two things:
remembrance and repentance. Remembrance includes recall-
ing the past, acknowledging its influence in the present, and
appropriating it as a resource when in fact it is resourceful. In
the mainstream of the prophetic tradition, the criteria used to
evaluate the resourcefulness of the past are love and social
justice. Those aspects of the past that inspire love and justice
are worthy of repetition. They should be remembered and
appropriated. By contrast, those that inspire hatred and injustice require repentance.

In the biblical context, repentance is more than mere regret. It is a turning around of life: a transformation lured by
the image of how life can be lived in the future, as distinct
from how it has been lived in the past. Hence, repentance is a
forward-looking rather than a backward-looking process. It is
provoked by, but not bound to, a past that is remembered.
This means that the final stage of repentance is hope rather
than guilt. Individuals and societies repent when they hope
that, in the future, things can be different from the way they
have been in the past.

If, as I suggest, certain aspects of the Christian heritage are
destructive rather than constructive, then the prophetic tradition invites a process of turning around, or repentance, on

the part of contemporary Christians. As individuals composing a global community called the church, Christians can and should turn around from those aspects of the past that yield war rather than peace, injustice rather than justice, and environmental destruction rather than ecological balance. In some instances this will involve repenting from aspects of the past that are embodied in the Bible itself. Certain aspects of the Jewish Bible, for example, are unjust with respect to women; certain aspects of the New Testament are unjust with respect to Jews; and certain aspects of both scriptural traditions are unjust with respect to the natural world and other religious traditions. In the interests of peace, justice, and sustainability, and in responsiveness to the God who continually calls toward new and hopeful futures, these aspects of the biblical past must be transcended.

But it is not the biblical past that is of foremost concern in this essay. Despite its destructive components, the biblical heritage contains much that inspires a prophetic pursuit of peace, justice, and sustainability. Of concern in this essay, instead, is the mythic vision in terms of which even the most constructive aspects of the Bible have sometimes been articulated. This world view is that of substantialism. If Christianity is to be of service to the global future, it must transcend its substantialist past.

The Substantialist Perspective

The substantialist perspective involves thinking about the self, the world, and God on the analogy of lifeless objects of detached sense perception: objects such as rocks, cups and saucers, metal levers, or billiard balls. Although substantialism existed long before the invention of billiards, it can best be understood by taking billiard balls as a paradigm case. This is because billiard balls, as ordinarily conceived by the unscientific observer, are analogous to "substances," as the latter have been envisioned in the Western imagination. In effect, Christianity has often rendered unto the self, the world, and God that which belongs to billiard balls.

For purposes of illustration, imagine a table on which lies a collection of billiard balls. Each ball represents a distinct entity of some sort: organic or inorganic, human or nonhuman, macroscopic or microscopic. One ball might be an atom, another a plant, another a nonhuman animal, and another a human being. Standing over the table is a pool player with cue in hand, representing God. My argument is that billiard balls, as ordinarily conceived, possess three properties which, taken individually or collectively, have often been assigned to entities within the world, and even to God.

Self-Containment

The first property is self-containment. A billiard ball lying on the table is contained within itself, cut off from other balls by the boundaries of its surface. The other balls are not part of its internal essence, and it is not part of theirs. Mutual externality, rather than mutual interfusion, is the nature of billiard-ball relationships.

In the popular imagination during much of the Christian past, the human self and God have been envisioned on the analogy of self-containment. The self has been envisioned as a self-contained soul locked within the body, cut off from the world by the boundaries of the skin. And God has been construed as a self-contained Lord residing in heaven, cut off from the world by the boundaries of divine transcendence. At times, of course, Christians have talked about divine immanence. But more often than not, this immanence has been conceived as the intervention of a self-contained agent who approaches the self and world from afar, rather than the omnipresence of a living Spirit in whose life the world and self are included. God and the human self have rarely been viewed as co-inhering and interdependent realities, except in the singular instance of Jesus. From the perspective of traditional Christianity, the incarnation of God in Jesus is an exception to, rather than an expression of, the nature of the divine-human relationship.

Moreover, both God and the human soul have each been conceived as self-contained in relation to the physical world. While the physical world has been seen as a creation of God, it has not been viewed as part of God's own nature. And while the human soul has been viewed as inhabiting a physical body, it has not been viewed as a physical reality in its own right. God and the soul have been viewed as spiritual substances, to be distinguished from the natural world, which consists of material substances. Philosophically, this is the infamous perspective of Descartes. But Descartes was simply expressing a deep-seated mythical heritage that long preceded him, and that has long succeeded him.

Hence, the presupposition of self-containment has resulted in at least three dichotomies that have pervaded the mythical heritage of the Christian past. The first is a dichotomy between soul and the world. When humans think in such terms, the world is naturally approached as an "other" to be manipulated or transcended, rather than as a potential "home" in which to dwell. The result is a self-imposed alienation from the world on the one hand, and social irresponsibility on the other. Of course, there is much in the world today from which people rightly feel alienated—poverty, repression, ecological destruction, and the threat of nuclear war—but the solution to these problems must involve the idea that the world can be a home in which to dwell. Social responsibility begins with an awareness that, for good or ill, the world is part of the self. The dichotomy between soul and world thwarts such awareness.

The second dichotomy that results from an emphasis on

self-containment is between God and the world. When humans think in such terms, God is imaged either as an aloof observer of worldly events or as a manipulative agent whose methods are coercion and force. To use the analogy from billiards, God emerges as a pool player who watches the movements of the balls from afar or who intervenes from time to time by striking balls with a cue. This way of thinking about God thwarts a realization of divine suffering with and in the world, and it encourages the view that God is a holy warrior whose power is that of external force. Christians who think of God in such terms can easily become dispassionate spectators or holy warriors themselves. In light of the threat of nuclear war, neither detached passivity nor dogmatic belligerence can meet the needs of the global future.

The third dichotomy is between the spiritual and the material. When this dichotomy reigns, the "material world" is inevitably abused, along with everything that is symbolically identified with it. In the mythical heritage of Christianity, for example, the rights of nonhuman nature have been disregarded, sexuality has been desacralized, and women (who have often been identified with nature and sexuality) have been victimized. Equally as problematic, problems of poverty and the inequitable distribution of material goods have been dismissed as less important than "spiritual" needs. Clearly, in a world that seeks ecological sustainability and social justice, the dichotomy between the spiritual and material must be transcended. The biblical emphasis on a prophetic pursuit of global justice must be revisioned in non-substantialist terms.

Can Christianity open itself to a process of revisionment? Unfortunately, another aspect of the substantialist heritage cuts against an openness to change. In addition to the idea of self-containment, there has been an excessive emphasis on immutability.

Immutability

As we observe a billiard ball moving from one region of a pool table to another, we ordinarily assume that the ball remains identical with itself over time. It moves, but its internal constitution does not change. Of course, physics and chemistry tell us the contrary. They tell us that the ball consists of molecules and atoms that are in a state of constant flux. But we do not see it this way. We see the ball as remaining unchanged with respect to time. It is a being devoid of becoming.

In much of the Christian past, Christianity itself has been conceived in precisely this fashion. It has been envisioned as a changeless tradition that moves through time, remaining self-identical amidst this movement. Sometimes the unchanging essence of Christianity has been identified with a particular set of creeds, sometimes with Scripture, and sometimes with Jesus of Nazareth. But in each case the essence has been interpreted as something immutable or unchanging. Rarely has the essence of Christianity itself been construed as an ongoing process—a process in which Christians are invited to be open to possibilities for new vision.

Accompanying this emphasis on the immutability of tradition has been an emphasis on the immutability of God. Despite biblical images of God as one who is influenced by, and responsive to, worldly events as they occur, most Christian theologians before the nineteenth century envisioned God as utterly changeless. For both Augustine and Aquinas, God was pure being, devoid of temporality or process. Time was construed as a product of God's creation, but not as part of the divine life. At a popular level, this emphasis on divine immutability has been expressed in ordinary assumptions that the details of the future are known by God in advance because "he" is "beyond time." The problems of reconciling this view with human freedom are notorious, as are the problems of reconciling classical theological images of God as pure being with the biblical image of a temporally responsive deity.

In the life of the church, the two emphases on divine immutability and ecclesiastical immutability have reinforced one another. The result has often been an inflexibility on the part of Christians to calls for change. At an intellectual level, this inflexibility has been reflected in resistance to the insights of modern science, biblical scholarship, and secular modes of thought. At a social level, it has been reflected in resistance to calls for social change that might yield peace, justice, and sustainability, and at an imaginative level, it has been reflected in an unwillingness to be open to new vision. Despite the biblical axiom quoted at the beginning of this essay, the traditional emphasis on immutability has resulted in a mythical perspective that has often been backward-looking rather than forward-looking. Again, substantialism emerges as an obstacle to the global future.

Instrumentality

The third aspect of substantialist thinking that has characterized much Christian thought concerns value. It is the idea that entities within the world are mere facts, devoid of intrinsic value, until assigned value by an external observer. As a pool player gazes upon billiard balls lying on a table, for example, the player ordinarily assumes that the balls have no value in and for themselves. They are mere objects—bare physical facts—with instrumental value and nothing more. Their value lies in their usefulness.

An overriding emphasis on instrumental or assigned value can be seen in two aspects of the Christian mythical heritage. In the first place, the value of human life has often been approached entirely in terms of its instrumentality to God's purposes. Humans have thought of themselves as bare facts, devoid of value, until assigned worth by God. As Nietzsche pointed out, and as feminist theologians have increasingly insisted, this emphasis on obsequiousness before God has resulted in a slavish mentality that has thwarted wholesome self-affirmation. It has given rise to the oppressive idea that all goodness comes from God and all evil from the world.

In the second place, a stress on instrumental value has influenced the way in which humans have approached non-human nature. Nature has been approached almost exclusively in terms of its instrumental value to human ends, rather than in terms of its intrinsic value, that is, its value in and for itself. Nature, too, has been conceived as bare fact, devoid of value.

Clearly, something is important about the idea of instrumental value. Human beings are in fact useful to one another and perhaps also to God. Likewise, the natural world is in fact useful to human beings and perhaps also to God. Without an instrumental approach to the environment, neither humans nor nonhumans could survive. Perhaps not even God could survive.

And yet, as Martin Buber pointed out in his classic *I and Thou*, an instrumental approach to the environment is not enough. The compassionate life involves an ability to see things in their intrinsic value, in their value for themselves as well as their value for others. This is to see something as a "Thou" rather than an "It." It is to recognize that "facts" on the outside are "values" on the inside. And it is to recognize that this inner value is the actuality itself, from its own perspective.

Although the mythical heritage of the Christian past has often encouraged a recognition of the worth of other human beings, and sometimes even of nonhuman nature, this worth has usually been interpreted as that which is assigned by God from without, rather than that which emerges from a being from within. It is value as created by God, analogous to a coat of paint applied to a valueless billiard ball.

If human beings are to find within themselves the re-sources for peace, justice, and sustainability, they must learn to recognize that all living beings, human and nonhuman, have intrinsic as well as instrumental value. This means that the idea of bare instrumentality must itself be over-come, perhaps even at the level of billiard balls. And if Christians are to be responsive to the global need for overcoming an exclusive emphasis on instrumentality, they too, must be open to possibilities for new vision.

An Ecological Alternative

Substantialism did not begin with the invention of billiards in the sixteenth century. It began when men around the world took passive objects of detached sense perception, and in particular visual perception, as models for understanding the nature of reality. Just as rocks and artifacts appeared static and disconnected when visually scrutinized from a de-tached perspective, so the ultimate units of reality—whether invisible "essences" or material "objects"—were thought to be static and disconnected. In the West, as Heidegger has pointed out, the origins of this epistemologi-cal procedure lie in Greek philosophy. Consciously or un-consciously, many Greek thinkers took visual experience as the primary point of departure for their ruminations con-cerning the nature of things. This does not mean that they reduced reality to that which can be seen with the eyes. It does mean, however, that they conceived of nonvisible real-ities on the analogy of visible objects. The Platonists con-ceived of the invisible soul as if it were a self-enclosed object locked within the body and cut off from the physical world. The Aristotelians conceived of the divine as a self-enclosed object locked within itself and similarly isolated. The divine was an Unmoved Mover, and the soul was its human counterpart. Hence, the roots of substantialism in the Christian past lie, in part, in the appropriation of Greek modes of thought early in Christian history.

But the roots lie elsewhere as well. As every student of theology knows, the way of thinking of the Christian past has not only been Hellenistic; it has been patriarchal. With a few exceptions, the people who have shaped and controlled the mythic past of Christianity have been men rather than women. A nonexhaustive list of the dominant myth shapers of the past would include Paul, Augustine, Aquinas, Luther, Calvin, Schleiermacher, Kierkegaard, and, more recently, Barth, Tillich, Bultmann, Rahner, and Lonergan. A list of philosophers who have influenced Christian thought would appear the same: Plato, Aristotle, Descartes, Kant, Hegel, Nietzsche, and, more recently, existentialist thinkers. The history of philosophy has been as dominated by men as has the history of theology, and both have had a deep-seated impact on the Christian mythic heritage.

As feminist theologians have pointed out, this patriarchal approach to mythic vision has had disastrous consequences for both women and men. It has enslaved women to men, and it has enslaved men to oppressive images of masculinity. In addition, patriarchy has been at the root of Christian and Western insensitivity to the natural world. For a patriarchal approach to mythic vision underlies the dichotomy between "man" and "nature" that is characteristic of the substantialist heritage. Inasmuch as men have been in exclusive control of the myths, women have been identified with nature, and both women and nature have been subjected to male domination. In addition to Greek philosophy, then, patriarchy must be identified as a source of the substantialist vision of the past.

In light of these two roots of substantialism, it is clear that an alternative vision within Christianity must be, in certain crucial respects, post-Hellenistic and post-patriarchal. Yet, such a vision would not necessarily be unbiblical. Instead, it would appropriate biblical themes from a point of view that differs from the dominant substantialist heritage. For example, biblical emphases on the worth of the human self could be appropriated, but not from a perspective in which the self is viewed as an isolated substance locked within the body. Prophetic emphases on social justice could be appropriated, but not from a perspective in which male domination is deemed socially just. The emergence of new vision must involve a new hermeneutic, a new lens through which the biblical past is approached and interpreted.

In some instances, of course, biblical literature must itself be transcended. Yet, even a transcendence of biblical thinking is not necessarily unbiblical, for the prophetic strand of biblical thinking points beyond itself toward a God who calls for repentance as well as remembrance, for change as well as repetition, for a critical attitude toward the past as well as an appreciation of it. To move beyond biblical modes of thinking, once they are understood in light of historical and critical scholarship, can itself be biblical, if such movement occurs in fidelity to the God of love and justice to whom the Bible most persistently points. When biblical literature enjoins attitudes that are patriarchal, ecologically irresponsible, or war-inducing, these attitudes must be remembered, but not repeated. A new vision for the Christian future must involve a transcendence of bibliolatry, and therein will lie its appreciation of the Bible.

In what areas, then, is new vision emerging? Where do we find examples of an ecological alternative to the substantialism of the past? Not surprisingly, one area is feminist theology. In recent decades women have been revisioning the Christian gospel from a perspective that takes into account their own experience and insights, and the result is a way of looking at the world that moves beyond the dichotomy between "man" and "nature" that has haunted our heritage. While there is a great deal of diversity within feminist literature, the emergent vision is consistently ecological rather than substantialist, since it emphasizes the radical interdependence of all forms of life, the value of nonhuman life for itself, and the value of life itself as an ongoing process in which women, men, and the natural world creatively participate.

A second area of new vision is liberation theology. This style of thinking originates from the perspective of those who suffer from political and economic oppression, and for whom the "good news" of Christianity involves God's call for a liberation from this oppression. More often than not, liberation perspectives are emerging in Latin American, Native American, African, Asian, and North American contexts that are non-white and nonaffluent. While, again, there is a great deal of diversity within liberation theology, and while the emphases of some thinkers are focused more exclusively on problems of human ecology than on the human relationship with nonhuman nature, the vision that is emerging is more ecological than substantialistic. The dichotomy between spiritual concerns and material needs is transcended in light of a more holistic understanding of the world.

A third area in which new vision is emerging is process theology, which is influenced by the non-substantialist perspective of the philosopher Alfred North Whitehead. It is this style of theology on which I now focus, taking it as a paradigm instance of ecological thinking within contemporary Christian thought. My choice of process thought, however, should not suggest that feminist and liberation perspectives are less important. On the contrary, the process perspective, while perhaps offering the most systematic vision of an ecological alternative to substantialism, is in great need of enrichment from feminist and liberation perspectives if its sociopolitical implications are to be unpacked. A new mythic vision for the Christian future may well involve a synthesis of feminist, liberation, and process theologies, accompanied by an openness to mythic visions that arise out of non-Christian contexts. Fortunately, there are thinkers, such as John B. Cobb, Jr., Marjorie Suchocki, Delwin Brown, and Sheila Greeve Davaney, who embody such syntheses.[4]

Taking our cue from thinkers such as these, we can ask, How would an ecological mode of Christian thought differ from that of substantialism? The answer lies in considering the three emphases of substantialism—self-containment, immutability, and instrumentality—and asking, What would it be like to envision the self, the world, and God in light of their opposites? What would it be like, for example, to emphasize self-inclusion rather than self-containment; process rather than immutability; and intrinsic value rather than instrumentality? In order to illustrate these ideas, consider the example of a single human life, say that of a woman living in the United States, wife and mother in an urban setting.

Self-Inclusion

If we consider who the woman is—as a *self*—we see that her identity includes, rather than excludes, her relationships with other human beings. Her children and husband are part of who and what she is, as are her friends, her neighbors, those with whom she comes in contact on a daily basis, and those who are part of a public interest group she has recently joined. In addition, those whom she has known in the past are part of her identity, including her parents, her friends, and former schoolmates, as are those, in a different way, whom she imagines knowing in the future. Indeed, directly or indirectly, the entire human family, past, present, and future, is part of her identity. Her self cannot be imaged as a self-contained soul cut off from the world by the boundaries of her skin. People who are outside the body are within her self.

This principle of inclusion applies to nonhuman nature as well. Through the food she eats, the land on which her house resides, the flora and fauna that inhabit that land, the materials that compose her house, and the energy she uses, the natural world is part of her identity. Indeed, her own body is the most immediate region in which, directly or indirectly, the entire natural world is included within her identity. Her self is an en-peopled self, an embodied self, and an en-natured self.

From the ecological perspective of process thought, this inclusion of the world within the constitution of a self is exemplified in any and every actuality, whether it is a human being, an animal, a plant, a living cell, a molecule, or an atom. Each actuality is a self that enfolds the entire universe into its own nature. This does not mean that actualities are interchangeable. Each actuality enfolds the universe from a particular point of view that is unique to itself. The way in which the universe enters into the particular woman described above, for example, is different from the way in which it enters into the constitution of her husband or a single cell. Hence, each actuality is a *unique* synthesis of relationships to the world.

The implications of this idea for Christianity are threefold. Self-inclusion implies, in the first place, that solidarity with the world is a more appropriate attitude toward life than disengagement from the world. Christians can love their neighbors as themselves because in a very important sense their neighbors *are* themselves. The idea of self-inclusion implies, in the second place, that it is the world—the entire ecosystem—that merits an attitude of solidarity, rather than simply a human community, the nation, or the church. This does not mean that human communities, nations, and churches cannot be appreciated. It does mean, however, that they cannot provide the ultimate frame of reference in terms of which the rest of the world is to be evaluated. The planet as a whole is the fundamental social context in terms of which individual Christians must think, feel, and act.

The third implication of the idea of self-inclusion for Christians concerns God. From a relational or self-inclusivist perspective, the divine Spirit is not a disengaged observer whose primary preoccupation is with reward and punishment. Instead, God is a nurturing self in whose ongoing life the world is included. The universe itself, with its tragedy and its joy, is God's body. This means that the suffering of Jesus on the cross did not simply *represent* the suffering of God. It *was* the suffering of God, as is any and every instance of suffering. And it means that resurrections, whenever and wherever they occur, are part of God as well. What happens in and to the global ecosystem happens in and to God.

Hence, violations of humanity and nature are tragic in God's life, just as they are tragic in the lives of those who suffer their consequences. The hope for a sane, humane, and ecological future is a hope for God, just as it is a hope for the world. The power of God lies in an ever present call for peace, justice, and sustainability. The task of Christians, and of course of all human beings, is to respond to this call.

Process

The second idea that is central to an ecological perspective is that of process. Returning to the example of the woman, we realize that her life is not a settled and finished fact defined by its past, but rather an ongoing process of becoming in which she is continually making decisions that affect her future. At times, these decisions seem dramatic, as when she decided to become active in the public interest group, or when she decided to marry her husband, or to have children. At other times, they are more mundane. But each waking moment of her life involves an actualization of certain possibilities, and through these actualizations she creates herself. Her life is determined, not only by the world to which she is related, but by her actualization of possibilities in response to this world.

From the ecological point of view of process thought, the life of any and every actuality is an ongoing process of actualizing possibilities in response to the world. This is true of an animal, a living cell in a plant, and even of submicroscopic processes in the depths of atoms. An actuality is not simply what it has been in the past, it is also what it can be in the future. It is always in a process of actualizing possibilities for becoming what it can be. At the submicroscopic level, this creativity is for the most part nonconscious, and perhaps this is the case with living cells as well. But in the final analysis the actualities of the universe are creative processes rather than static facts. Human freedom is a sophisticated expression of, rather than an exception to, a creativity that is inherent in the nature of things.

What might this emphasis on creative process mean for Christians? At least three things. It could mean, in the first place, that Christianity itself is best conceived as an ongoing process rather than a settled fact. It could mean, in the second place, that the process of living itself, is the ultimate locus of value in human and nonhuman life. In keeping with the traditional understanding of the significance of Jesus' resurrection, Christians might think of the process of living for human and nonhuman life as continuing in some way after physical death. But in life after death, as in this life, it would be the process itself, rather than a static end, that would be emphasized. The value of being lies in its becoming.

Third, this emphasis on process could mean a transformation of our vision of God. Whereas much of the post-biblical past has envisioned God as an immutable absolute devoid of process, an ecological emphasis on process opens the door for a rediscovery of the biblical sensitivity that God is in process, along with the world. This does not mean that the character of God changes: that God is at one moment hate-filled, for example, and at another moment loving. It does mean, however, that the unending love of God is itself in process with the world, receiving the world into the divine essence at any and every moment, and responding to the world by availing it of possibilities for growth and development relative to the situation. The future is open for God as for the world. God is involved in, rather than detached from, the world's adventure of becoming.

Intrinsic Value

The final idea that is central to an ecological alternative to substantialism is that of intrinsic value. To return to the example of the woman, we see that her life involves a kind of value that cannot be reduced to that which is assigned to her by her husband and children. In addition to being valuable for them, she is valuable to and for herself. Moreover, she realizes the danger of thinking of her value solely in terms of her instrumentality. The consequences of defining herself entirely in terms of her usefulness to others are disastrous, both for herself and sometimes for them. In choosing to become part of a public interest group, for example, she is acting, not only for the sake of those whom she can help, but also for the sake of her own psychological well-being, for the sake of her own intrinsic value.

In the context of the ecological vision of process thought,

this idea of intrinsic value is applicable in relation to all living beings. Each and every organism has intrinsic value, or value in and for itself, as well as instrumental value, or value for others. The implications of this for environmental ethics are obvious. Although human survival inevitably involves the taking of life, careful deliberations must be made with respect to the circumstances of deprivation, for all life has intrinsic value. Ethical considerations must be biocentric rather than anthropocentric.

In addition to recognizing the intrinsic value of all forms of life, however, Christians who think ecologically must overcome the dogmatism of thinking that Christianity itself is the one true religion. A recognition of intrinsic value involves a realization that there are diverse forms of value and that diversity itself is valuable. Other religious traditions embody styles of living with distinctive value: value that is different from, rather than inferior to, Christian forms of life. A mythic vision that involves the idea of intrinsic value encourages, rather than discourages, a nurturing of diverse forms of human and nonhuman life.

Finally, the idea of intrinsic value implies a new understanding of God. Rather than thinking of God as one who assigns value from without, God can be conceived as one who inspires value from within. In actualizing possibilities availed by the divine Spirit, living beings create and express their own intrinsic value. God does not create the intrinsic value of living beings, as if these beings were bare facts devoid of value before divine assessment. Instead God inspires living beings toward enriched realizations of their own value in relation to the world. Intrinsic value is itself the way in which, from its own perspective, a living being includes the world within itself. In the final decades of the twentieth century, Christians can rightly assume that the call of God is toward forms of value realization that are peaceful, just, and sustainable. It is precisely these modes of self-creation that are most conducive to the preservation of diverse forms of intrinsic value.

Can the Christian tradition evolve beyond its substantialist heritage toward an ecological future? I suggest that it can. Although a transition of this sort involves a good deal of revisionment beyond what has been discussed, such revisionment is already occurring in process, liberation, and feminist perspectives. New images of Christ, the church, and the nature of Christian life are emerging. Still a question remains: *Will* this new ecological perspective become part of the practice of significant numbers of ordinary Christians around the world, so that they, as representatives of a worldwide community, can serve, rather than thwart, the needs of the global future? From an ecological perspective, the question cannot be answered. The future is not predetermined. The world, including the Christian tradition, is in process.

Notes

1. Lester Brown, *Building a Sustainable Society* (New York: W. W. Norton, 1981).
2. Robert C. Johanson, *The National Interest and the Human Interest: An Analysis of U.S. Foreign Policy* (Princeton, N.J.: Princeton University Press, 1980), p. 407.
3. Walter Brueggeman, *The Prophetic Imagination* (Philadelphia: Fortress Press, 1978), p. 45.
4. Charles Birch and John B. Cobb, Jr., *The Liberation of Life* (New York: Cambridge University Press, 1981); Delwin Brown, *To Set at Liberty* (Maryknoll, N.Y.: Orbis Books, 1981); Sheila Greeve Davaney, ed., *Feminism and Process Thought* (New York: Edward Mellen Press, 1981); Marjorie Suchocki, *God, Christ, Church* (New York: Crossroad, 1982).

Selected Bibliography

Attfield, Robin. *The Ethics of Environmental Concern.* New York: Columbia University Press, 1983.

Austin, Richard Cartwright. "Beauty: A Foundation for Environmental Ethics." *Environmental Ethics* 7 (1985):197–208.

Baer, Richard A. "Higher Education: The Church and Environmental Values." *Natural Resources Journal* 17 (1977):477–91.

Barbour, Ian G., ed. *Earth Might be Fair: Reflections on Ethics, Religion, and Ecology.* Englewood Cliffs, N.J.: Prentice-Hall, 1972.

———. *Technology, Environment, and Human Values.* New York: Praeger Publishers, 1980.

———. *Western Man and Environmental Ethics.* Menlo Park: Addison-Wesley, 1973.

Barker, Edwin, ed. *The Responsible Church.* London: S.P.C.K., Holy Trinity Church, 1966.

Barnette, Henlee H. *The Church and the Ecological Crisis.* Grand Rapids, Mich.: Eerdmans, 1972.

Berry, Thomas. *Teilhard in the Ecological Age.* Chambersburg, Pa.: Anima, 1982.

Birch, Charles, and John B. Cobb, Jr. *The Liberation of Life: From the Cell to the Community.* Cambridge: Cambridge University Press, 1981.

Blackstone, William T., ed. *Philosophy and Environmental Crisis.* Athens: University of Georgia Press, 1972.

Blidstein, Gerald J. "Man and Nature in the Sabbatical Year." *Tradition* 9 (1966):48–55.

Bonafazi, Conrad. "Biblical Roots of an Ecological Conscience." In *This Little Planet,* ed. M. Hamilton, pp. 203–33. New York: Charles Scribner's Sons, 1970.

_____. *The Soul of the World: An Account of the Inwardness of Things.* Lanham, Md.: University Press of America, 1978.

_____. *A Theology of Things.* New York and Philadelphia: Lippincott, 1967.

Bratton, Susan Power. "The Ecotheology of James Watt." *Environmental Ethics* 5 (1983):225–36.

Brueggemann, Walter. *The Land.* Philadelphia: Fortress Press, 1977.

Callicott, J. Baird. "Traditional American Indian and Western European Attitudes Toward Nature: An Overview." *Environmental Ethics* 4 (1984):293–318.

Carmody, John. *Ecology and Religion: Toward a Christian Theology of Nature.* New York: Paulist Press, 1983.

Cobb, John B., Jr. *Is It Too Late? A Theology of Ecology.* Beverly Hills, Calif.: Bruce, 1972.

Dalton, Mary A. "The Theology of Ecology: An Interdisciplinary Concept." *Religious Education* 71, no. 1 (1976):17–26.

Davies, W. D. *The Gospel and the Land: Early Christianity and Jewish Territorial Doctrine.* Berkeley: University of California Press, 1974.

Derr, Thomas S. *Barriers to Ecumenism: The Holy See and the World Council of Churches on Social Questions.* Maryknoll, N.Y.: Orbis Books, 1983.

_____. "Religion's Responsibility for the Ecological Crisis: An Argument Run Amok." *Worldview* 18, no. 1 (1975):39–45.

De Wolf, L. Harold. *Responsible Freedom: Guidelines to Christian Action.* New York: Harper and Row, 1971.

Ditmanson, Harold H. "The Call for a Theology of Creation." *Dialog* 3 (1964):264–73.

Dubos, René. *The Wooing of the Earth.* New York: Charles Scribner's Sons, 1980.

Ehrenfeld, David, and Bentley, Philip J. "Judaism and the Practice of Stewardship." *Judaism* 34 (1985):301–11.

Elder, Frederick. *Crisis in Eden: A Religious Study of Man and Environment.* New York: Abingdon Press, 1970.

Elliott, Robert, and Arran Gare, eds. *Environmental Philosophy: A Collection of Readings.* University Park: Pennsylvania State University Press, 1983.

Elsdon, Ron. *Bent World: A Christian Response to the Environmental Crisis.* Downers Grove, Ill.: InterVarsity Press, 1981.

Engel, David E. "Elements in a Theology of Environment." *Zygon* 5 (1970):216–28.

Ferré, Frederick. *Shaping the Future: Resources for the Post-modern World.* New York: Harper and Row, 1976.

Freudenberger, C. Dean. *Food for Tomorrow?* Minneapolis: Augsburger Publishing House, 1984.

Freudenstein, Eric C. "Ecology and the Jewish Tradition." *Judaism* 19 (1970):406–14.

Fritsch, Albert J. *Environmental Ethics: Choices for Concerned Citizens.* Garden City, N.Y.: Anchor Press, 1980.

Gilkey, Langdon. *Maker of Heaven and Earth.* New York: Doubleday, 1959.

Gillespie, Charles Coulston. *Genesis and Geology: A Study in the Relations of Scientific Thought, Natural Theology, and Social Opinion in Great Britain, 1790–1850.* Cambridge: Harvard University Press, 1951.

Glacken, Clarence J. *Traces on the Rhodian Shore.* Berkeley: University of California Press, 1967.

Goodman, Russell. "Taoism and Ecology." *Environmental Ethics* 2 (1980):73–80.

Gordis, Robert. "Judaism and the Spoliation of Nature." *Congress Bi-Weekly,* 2 April 1971.

Graber, Linda H. *Wilderness as Sacred Space.* Washington, D.C.: Association of American Geographers, 1976.

Granberg-Michaelson, Wesley. *A Worldly Spirituality: The Call to Take Care of the Earth.* New York: Harper and Row, 1984.

Gray, Elizabeth Dodson. *Green Paradise Lost.* Wellesley, Mass.: Roundtable Press, 1981. [An earlier edition was published in 1979 by the same publisher under the title, *Why the Green Nigger? Re-Mything Genesis.*]

Hamilton, Michael, ed. *This Little Planet.* New York: Charles Scribner's Sons, 1970.

Hargrove, Eugene C. "The Historical Foundations of American Environmental Attitudes." *Environmental Ethics* 1 (1979): 209–40.

Selected Bibliography

Hart, John. *The Spirit of the Earth: A Theology of the Land.* New York: Paulist Press, 1984.

Heiss, Richard L., and Noel F. McInnis, eds. *Can Man Care for the Earth?* New York: Abingdon Press, 1976.

Helfand, Jonathan. "Ecology and the Jewish Tradition: A Postscript." *Judaism* 20 (1971):330–35.

Hendry, George S. *Theology of Nature.* Philadelphia: Westminster Press, 1980.

Hessel, Dieter T., ed. *Energy Ethics: A Christian Response.* New York: Friendship Press, 1979.

Hughes, J. Donald. *American Indian Ecology.* El Paso: Texas Western Press, 1983.

———. *Ecology in Ancient Civilization.* Albuquerque: University of New Mexico Press, 1975.

Hurst, J. S. "Towards a Theology of Conservation." *Theology* 75 (1972):197–205.

Huth, Hans. *Nature and the American: Three Centuries of Changing Attitudes.* Berkeley: University of California Press, 1957.

Jegen, Mary Evelyn, and Bruno Manno, eds. *The Earth is the Lord's: Essays on Stewardship.* New York: Paulist Press, 1978.

Joranson, Philip N., and Ken Butigan, eds. *Cry of the Environment: Rebuilding the Christian Creation Tradition.* Sante Fe, N.Mex.: Bear, 1984.

Klostermaier, Klaus. "World Religions and the Ecological Crisis." *Religion* 3, no. 2 (1973):132–45.

Kohák, Erazim. *The Embers and the Stars: A Philosophical Inquiry into the Moral Sense of Nature.* Chicago: University of Chicago Press, 1984.

Krolzik, Udo. *Umweltkrise—Folge des Christentums?* 2nd ed. Stuttgart and Berlin: Kreuz Verlag, 1979.

Kultgen, John. "Saving *You* for Real People." *Environmental Ethics* 4 (1982):59–67.

Lamm, Norman. "The Earth is the Lord's." In *Judaism and Human Rights,* ed. Milton R. Konvitz. New York: W. W. Norton, 1972.

———. "Ecology in Jewish Law and Theology." in *Faith and Doubt.* New York: Ktav, 1971.

Leiss, William. *The Domination of Nature.* Boston: Beacon Press, 1972.

Linzey, Andrew. *Animal Rights: A Christian Assessment of Man's Treatment of Animals.* London: SCM Press, 1976.

Lutz, Paul, and Paul H. Santmire. *Ecological Renewal.* Philadelphia: Fortress Press, 1972.

Martin, Calvin. *Keepers of the Game: Indian-Animal Relationship and the Fur Trade.* Berkeley and Los Angeles: University of California Press, 1978.

McDaniel, Jay. "Christian Spirituality as Openness to Fellow Creatures." *Environmental Ethics* 8 (1986):33–46.

Midgley, Mary. *Animals and Why They Matter.* Athens: University of Georgia Press, 1983.

Montefiore, Hugh, ed. *Man and Nature.* London: Collins, 1975.

Morris, Richard Knowles, and Michael W. Fox, eds. *On the Fifth Day.* Washington, D.C.: Acropolis Books, 1977.

Nash, Roderick. *Wilderness and the American Mind.* rev. 3rd ed. New Haven: Yale University Press, 1982.

Nibley, Hugh W. "On Subduing the Earth." In *Nibley on the Timely and the Timeless.* Salt Lake City, Utah: Publishers Press, 1978.

Nicolson, Marjorie Hope. *Mountain Gloom and Mountain Glory: The Development of the Aesthetic of the Infinite.* New York: W. W. Norton, 1963.

Overholt, Thomas, and J. Baird Callicott. *Clothed-in-Fur and Other Tales: An Introduction to the Ojibwa World View.* Washington, D.C.: University Press of America, 1982.

Partridge, Ernest, ed. *Responsibilities to Future Generations: Environmental Ethics.* Buffalo, N.Y.: Prometheus Books, 1981.

Passmore, John. *Man's Responsibility for Nature: Ecological Problems and Western Traditions.* New York: Charles Scribner's Sons, 1974.

Regan, Tom, and Peter Singer, eds. *Animal Rights and Human Obligations.* Englewood Cliffs, N.J.: Prentice-Hall, 1976.

———. "Environmental Ethics and the Ambiguity of the Native American Relationship with Nature." In *All That Dwell Therein.* Berkeley and Los Angeles: University of California Press, 1982.

Rolston, Holmes, III. *Philosophy Gone Wild: Essays in Environmental Ethics.* Buffalo, N.Y.: Prometheus Books, 1986.

Ruether, Rosemary Radford. *New Woman, New Earth: Sexist Ideologies & Human Liberation.* New York: Seabury Press, 1975.

Rust, Eric C. *Nature and Man in Biblical Thought*. London: Lutterworth Press, 1953.

_____. *Nature—Garden or Desert? An Essay on Environmental Theology*. Waco, Tex.: World Books, 1971.

Santmire, Paul H. *Brother Earth: Nature, God and Ecology in Time of Crisis*. New York: Thomas Nelson, 1970.

_____. *The Travail of Nature: The Ambiguous Ecological Promise of Christian Theology*. Philadelphia: Fortress Press, 1985.

Schaeffer, Francis A. *Pollution and the Death of Man: The Christian View of Ecology*. London: Hodder and Stoughton, 1970.

Schaffer, Arthur. "The Agricultural and Ecological Symbolism of the Four Species of Sukkot." *Tradition* 20 (1982):128–40.

Scherer, Donald, and Thomas Attig, eds. *Ethics and the Environment*. Englewood Cliffs, N.J.: Prentice-Hall, 1983.

Schueler, Robert L. "Ecology—The New Religion?" *America* 122, no. 11 (1970):292–95.

Schultz, Robert C., and J. Donald Hughes, eds. *Ecological Consciousness: Essays from the Earthday X Colloquium*. Washington, D.C.: University Press of America, 1981.

Schumacher, E. F. "Buddhist Economics." In *Small Is Beautiful*. New York: Harper and Row, 1975.

Schwarzchild, Steven S. "The Unnatural Jew." *Environmental Ethics* 6 (1984):347–62.

Shepard, Paul. *Nature and Madness*. San Francisco: Sierra Club Books, 1982.

Shepherd, J. Barrie. "Theology for Ecology." *Catholic World* 211 (July 1970):172–75.

Shinn, Roger L., ed. *Faith and Science in an Unjust World*. 2 vols. Philadelphia: Fortress Press, 1980.

Sider, Ronald J. *Living More Simply: Biblical Principles & Practical Models*. Downers Grove, Ill.: InterVarsity Press, 1980.

_____. *Rich Christians in an Age of Hunger: A Biblical Study*. Downers Grove, Ill.: InterVarsity Press, 1977.

Sikora, R. I., and Brian Barry, eds. *Obligations to Future Generations*. Philadelphia: Temple University Press, 1978.

Singer, Peter. *Animal Liberation: A New Ethics for Our Treatment of Animals*. New York: New York Review, 1975.

Sittler, Joseph. "Ecological Commitment as Theological Responsibility." *Zygon* 5 (1970):172–81.

――――. *Essays on Nature and Grace.* Philadelphia: Fortress Press, 1972.

――――. "A Theology for the Earth." *Christian Scholar* 37 (1954):367–74.

Skolimowski, Henryk. *Eco-Theology: Toward a Religion for Our Times.* Eco-Philosophy Publications, no. 2. Madras, India: Vasanta Press, 1985.

Spring, David, and Eileen Spring, eds. *Ecology and Religion in History.* New York: Harper and Row, 1974.

Squires, Edwin R., ed. *The Environmental Crisis: The Ethical Dilemma.* Mancelona, Mich.: AuSable Trails Institute of Environmental Studies, 1982.

Steffenson, Dave, Walter J. Herscher, and Robert S. Cook, eds. *Ethics for Environment: Three Religious Strategies.* Green Bay, Wis.: Green Bay Ecumenical Center, 1973.

Stefferud, Alfred, ed. *Christians and the Good Earth.* New York: Friendship Press, 1969.

Stivers, Robert L. *Hunger, Technology & Limits to Growth: Christian Responsibility for Three Ethical Issues.* Minneapolis: Augsburg Publishing House, 1984.

Stone, Glenn, ed. *A New Ethics for a New Earth.* New York: Friendship Press, 1971.

Stott, John R., ed. *The Year 2000.* Downers Grove, Ill.: InterVarsity Press, 1983.

Tallmadge, John. "Saying *You* to the Land." *Environmental Ethics* 3 (1981):251–63.

Toynbee, Arnold. "The Religious Background of the Present Environmental Crisis: A Viewpoint." *International Journal of Environmental Studies* 3, no. 2 (1972):141–46.

von Rad, Gerhard. *Genesis: A Commentary.* Philadelphia: Westminster Press, 1972.

Vorspan, Albert. "The Crisis of Ecology: Judaism and the Environment." In *Jewish Values and Social Crisis.* New York: Union of American Hebrew Congregations, 1970.

Westermann, Claus. *Creation.* Philadelphia: Fortress Press, 1974.

Selected Bibliography

_____. *Elements of Old Testament Theology.* Atlanta: John Knox Press, 1982.

_____. *Genesis 1–11: A Commentary.* Minneapolis: Augsburg Publishing House, 1984.

White, Lynn, Jr. "The Historical Roots of our Ecological Crisis." *Science* 155 (1967):1203–7.

Whitehead, Alfred North. *Science and the Modern World: Lowell Lectures, 1925.* New York: Free Press, 1967.

Wilkinson, Loren, ed. *Earthkeeping: Christian Stewardship of Natural Resources.* Grand Rapids, Mich.: Eerdmans, 1980.

Williams, George H. *Wilderness and Paradise in Christian Thought.* New York: Harper and Row, 1962.

Wood, Harold W., Jr. "Modern Pantheism as an Approach to Environmental Ethics." *Environmental Ethics* 7 (1985):151–63.

Young, R. V., Jr. "A Conservative View of Environmental Affairs." *Environmental Ethics* 1 (1979):241–54.

Contributors

ROBERT H. AYERS is a professor of religion at the University of Georgia.

SUSAN POWER BRATTON is the head of the National Park Service Cooperative Unit at the University of Georgia's Institute of Ecology.

JOHN B. COBB, JR., is a professor of theology at the School of Theology at Claremont.

FREDERICK FERRÉ is a professor of philosophy and the head of the Department of Philosophy and the Faculty of Environmental Ethics at the University of Georgia.

EUGENE C. HARGROVE is the editor of the journal *Environmental Ethics.*

JONATHAN HELFAND is an associate professor in the Department of Judaic Studies at Brooklyn College.

J. DONALD HUGHES is a professor of history at the University of Denver and a visiting professor of history at the University of Colorado, Boulder.

PO-KEUNG IP is the college secretary of Lingnan College in Hong Kong.

Contributors

SOPHIE JAKOWSKA is a member of the Education Commission of the International Union for the Conservation of Nature and Natural Resources.

MARTIN LABAR is a professor of science at Central Wesleyan College.

JAY MCDANIEL is an associate professor of religion and the director of the Marshall T. Steel Center for the Study of Religion and Philosophy at Hendrix College.

GERARD REED is a professor of history, philosophy, and religion at Point Loma Nazarene College.

IQTIDAR HUSAIN ZAIDI is a professor and chairman of the Department of Geography at the University of Karachi, Pakistan.